1st

Social Studies

Daily Practice Workbook

20 weeks of fun activities

ARGOPREP

Veterans Day

History • **Civics and Government** • **Geography** • **Economics**

ArgoPrep is one of the leading providers of supplemental educational products and services. We offer affordable and effective test prep solutions to educators, parents and students. Learning should be fun and easy! To access more resources visit us at www.argoprep.com.

Our goal is to make your life easier, so let us know how we can help you by e-mailing us at: info@argoprep.com.

- ArgoPrep is a recipient of the prestigious **Mom's Choice Award**.

- ArgoPrep also received the 2019 **Seal of Approval** from Homeschool.com for our award-winning workbooks.

- ArgoPrep was awarded the 2019 **National Parenting Products Award, Gold Medal Parent's Choice Award** and **the Tillywig Brain Child Award.**

SOCIAL STUDIES

Social Studies Daily Practice Workbook by ArgoPrep allows students to build foundational skills and review concepts. Our workbooks explore social studies topics in depth with ArgoPrep's 5 E's to build social studies mastery.

OTHER BOOKS BY ARGOPREP

Here are some other test prep workbooks by ArgoPrep you may be interested in. All of our workbooks come equipped with detailed video explanations to make your learning experience a breeze! Visit us at www.argoprep.com

COMMON CORE MATH SERIES

COMMON CORE ELA SERIES

INTRODUCING MATH!

Introducing Math! by ArgoPrep is an award-winning series created by certified teachers to provide students with high-quality practice problems. Our workbooks include topic overviews with instruction, practice questions, answer explanations along with digital access to video explanations. Practice in confidence - with ArgoPrep!

SCIENCE SERIES

Science Daily Practice Workbook by ArgoPrep is an award-winning series created by certified science teachers to help build mastery of foundational science skills. Our workbooks explore science topics in depth with ArgoPrep's 5 E'S to build science mastery.

KIDS SUMMER ACADEMY SERIES

ArgoPrep's Kids Summer Academy series helps prevent summer learning loss and gets students ready for their new school year by reinforcing core foundations in math, english and science. Our workbooks also introduce new concepts so students can get a head start and be on top of their game for the new school year!

WATER FIRE

MYSTICAL NINJA

GREEN POISON

FIRESTORM WARRIOR

RAPID NINJA

CAPTAIN ARGO

THUNDER WARRIOR

DANCE HERO

ADRASTOS THE SUPER WARRIOR

CAPTAIN BRAVERY

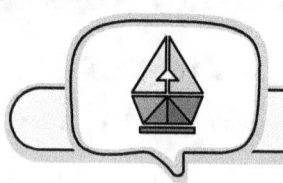
Introduction

Welcome to our first grade social studies workbook!

This workbook has been specifically designed to help students build mastery of foundational social studies skills that are taught in first grade. Included are 20 weeks of comprehensive instruction covering the four branches of social studies: History, Civics and Government, Geography, and Economics.

This workbook dedicates five weeks of instruction to each of the four branches of social studies, focusing on different standards within each week of instruction.

Within the branch of History, students will make connections between their own environment and the past. In Civics and Government, they will learn more about the rights and responsibilities of citizens. Students will dive into the physical and human features of their community in Geography. Finally, in the Economics section, they will have the opportunity to learn about different jobs, goods, and services.

At the conclusion of the 20 weeks of instruction, students should have a solid grasp of the concepts required by the National Council for Social Studies for first grade.

Table of Contents

How to Use the Book

All 20 weeks of daily activity pages in this book follow the same weekly structure. The book is divided into four sections: History, Civics and Government, Geography, and Economics. The activities in each of the sections align to the recommendations of the National Council for the Social Studies which will help prepare students for state standardized assessments. While the sections can be completed in any order, it is important to complete each week within the section in chronological order since the skills often build upon one another.

Each week focuses on one specific topic within the section. More information about the weekly structure can be found in the Weekly Planner section.

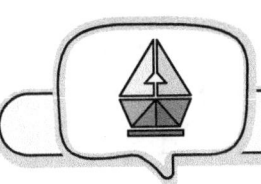
Weekly Planner

Day	Activity	Description
1	Engaging with the Topic	Read a short text on the topic and answer multiple choice questions.
2	Exploring the Topic	Interact with the topic on a deeper level by collecting, analyzing and interpreting information.
3	Explaining the Topic	Make sense of the topic by explaining and beginning to draw conclusions about information.
4	Experiencing the Topic	Investigate the topic by making real-life connections.
5	Elaborating on the Topic	Reflect on the topic and use all information learned to draw conclusions and evaluate results.

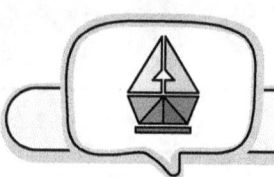
List of Topics

Unit	Week	Topic
History	1	Community Life: Past and Present
History	2	American Songs and Symbols
History	3	National Holidays
History	4	Timelines
History	5	American Folktales
Civics and Government	6	Rights and Responsibilities
Civics and Government	7	Rules and Laws
Civics and Government	8	The Common Good
Civics and Government	9	Being a Good Citizen
Civics and Government	10	The Pledge of Allegiance
Geography	11	Cardinal Directions
Geography	12	Physical vs. Human Features
Geography	13	Weather
Geography	14	Maps
Geography	15	Natural Resources
Economics	16	Goods
Economics	17	Services
Economics	18	Producers and Consumers
Economics	19	Scarcity
Economics	20	Jobs

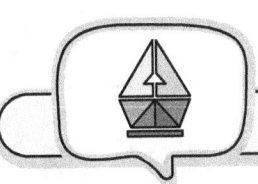
How to access video explanations?

Go to **argoprep.com/social1**
OR scan the QR Code:

WEEK 1

History

Community Life: Past and Present

Identify similarities and differences between the past and present in community life.

ARGOPREP

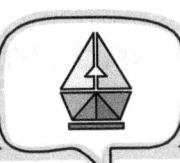
Directions: Read the text below. Then answer the questions that follow.

Life in the Past

A long time ago, many things were different from how they are now, while other things were similar. Houses and clothing looked different. Children played with different toys and games. However, just like today, adults went to work or cared for young children, and older children went to school.

1. Many things in the past were different from how they are now.

   A. True

   B. False

2. What types of things are similar now to how they were long ago? Circle two answers.

   A. Toys and games

   B. Houses

   C. Jobs

   D. School

3. Which of the following statements is true?

   A. Children did not have to go to school long ago.

   B. Houses and cars look the same now as they did long ago.

   C. The clothing we wear now looks similar to the clothing worn by people long ago.

   D. Grown-ups had jobs long ago, just as they do now.

Yesterday you learned about things that were similar and different about the past and present. Today you will explore what school was like in the past.

Directions: Read the text below. Then answer the questions that follow.

> Long ago, children went to school at a schoolhouse. Schoolhouses usually had one room full of desks and chairs for students. They also had books, pencils, paper, and a blackboard. Children of all ages learned together from one teacher. Many children had to travel far to get to school. Schools would often be closed during certain times of the year so that children could work on their family's farms.

Directions: In the table below, list things that are the same and different about schools of the past and present using the text above.

Same	Different

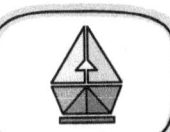
Yesterday you learned about the ways school was different in the past. Today you will explain how your school is the same or different from the school in the picture.

Directions Look at the picture below. Think of how your school is similar to the one in the picture. Then, think of how your school is different from the one in the picture. List your responses on the next page.

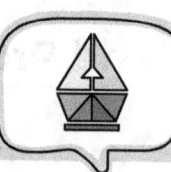
1. How is your school the SAME as the one in the picture?

....

....

....

....

....

2. How is your school DIFFERENT from the one in the picture?

....

....

....

....

....

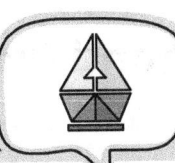
You have spent several days learning, exploring, and explaining how life was different in the past. Today you will compare and contrast how you travel to school with how children traveled to school in the past.

Directions: Read the text below. Then answer the questions that follow.

"

Many things have changed over time in our country besides schools. Long ago, people used different modes of transportation. There were no school buses to take children to school. Many had to walk long distances or take a buggy. A buggy is a carriage that is pulled by a horse. Very few people had cars to help them get around.

"

1. How did children get to school in the past?

   A. They rode a school bus.

   B. They walked.

   C. They rode in a car.

2. How do you get to school? Write your answer on the line below.

   ....

3. Do you get to school in the same way as children long ago or in a different way?

   A. Same

   B. Different

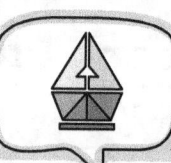
Yesterday you compared and contrasted life in the past and present. Today you will reflect on what life might have been like for children in the past.

Directions: Read and answer each question below.

1. Draw a picture of something that is the same now as it was in the past.

2. Draw a picture of something that is different now from how it was in the past.

WEEK 2

History

American Songs and Symbols

Identify American songs and symbols and discuss their origins.

ARGOPREP

Directions: Read the text below. Then answer the questions that follow.

What is a Symbol?

A **symbol** is something that represents something else. The United States of America has many different symbols that represent freedom and democracy. Symbols can be songs, flags, statues, or pictures. The Statue of Liberty, the American Flag, and the Bald Eagle are all important symbols of our country.

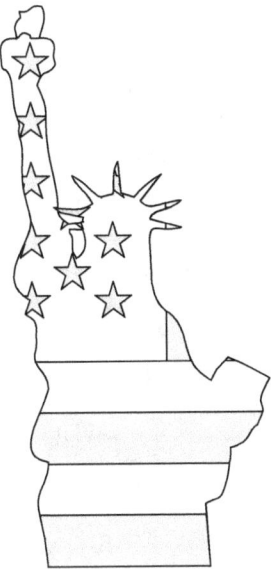

1. A symbol is something that represents something else.

    A. True

    B. False

2. Which of the following are American symbols? Circle all that apply.

    A. The White House

    B. The American Flag

    C. A cardinal

    D. The Statue of Liberty

3. The United States of America has only one important symbol.

    A. True

    B. False

4. Name another American symbol not listed above.

Yesterday you learned about symbols. Today you will explore a special symbol of our country, The Star-Spangled Banner.

Directions: Read the text below. Then answer the questions that follow.

The Star-Spangled Banner

The Star-Spangled Banner is our country's national anthem, meaning our national song. It was written as a poem by Francis Scott Key. He wrote it during the War of 1812. President Hoover signed a law in 1931 which made The Star-Spangled Banner the official national anthem of the United States.

1. The Star-Spangled Banner is a song.

   A. True

   B. False

2. Anthem is another word for:

   A. Poem

   B. Book

   C. Song

   D. Law

3. Which of the following statements is false?

   A. Francis Scott Key wrote The Star-Spangled Banner.

   B. The Star-Spangled Banner became the national anthem in 1812.

   C. The Star-Spangled Banner was originally written as a poem.

   D. The Star-Spangled Banner was written during the War of 1812.

4. Which president made The Star-Spangled Banner the national anthem of the United States?

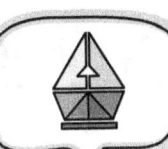
Yesterday you learned about The Star-Spangled Banner. Today you will explain how the White House is an American symbol.

Directions: Read the text below. Then answer the questions that follow.

"

The White House is where the President of the United States lives and works. It is located in Washington, D.C. The White House is full of many important paintings and other pieces of our country's history. Many people visit the White House every day.

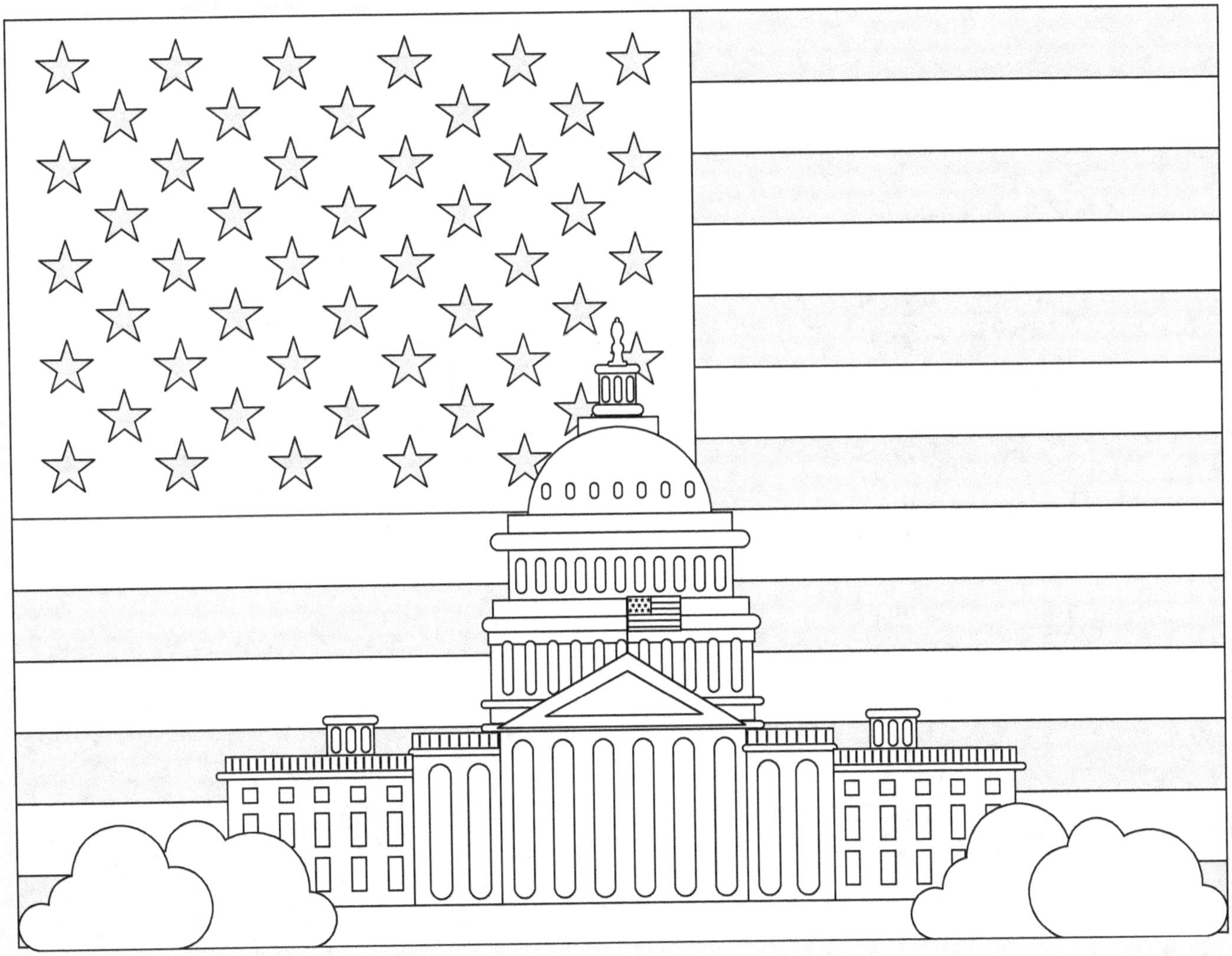

"

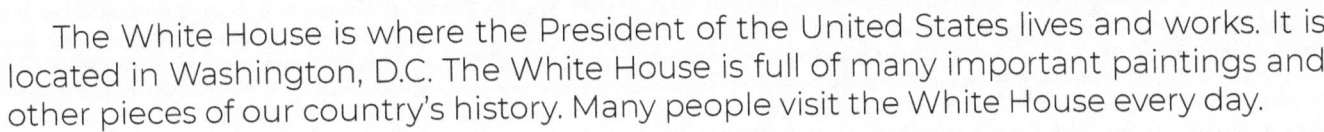

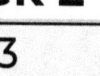
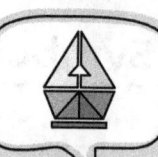
1. The White House is an important American symbol.

   A. True

   B. False

2. Complete the sentence below.

The White House is an important American symbol because

....

....

....

....

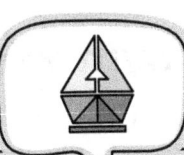
You have spent several days learning, exploring, and explaining important American symbols. Today you will decide which images show important American symbols and which do not.

Directions: Look at the pictures below. Then answer the questions that follow.

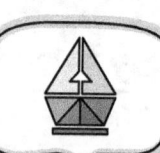
1. Circle the picture that does NOT show an important American symbol.

2. How do you know that is not an American symbol?

....

....

....

....

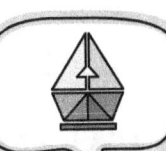
Yesterday you analyzed different pictures of American symbols. Today you will draw a picture of a different American symbol that you know.

Directions: Think of an American symbol. In the box below, draw a picture of it.

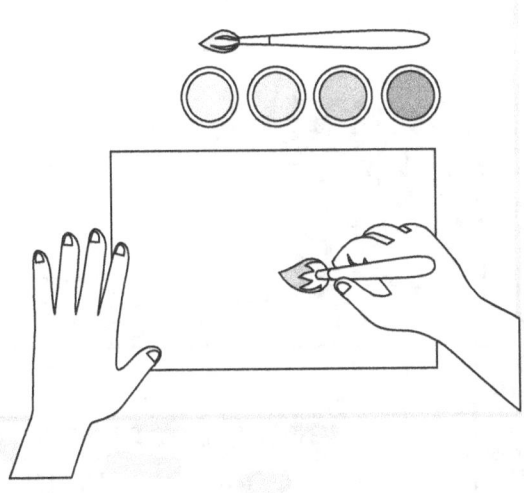

WEEK 3

History
National Holidays

Identify people and events observed on national celebrations and holidays.

Directions: Read the text below. Then answer the questions that follow.

What is a National Holiday?

A **national holiday** is a day recognized by the federal government as a day of celebration across the entire country. We celebrate many national holidays in the United States. Martin Luther King, Jr. Day, President's Day, Independence Day, and Veteran's Day are all examples of national holidays. On these holidays, many businesses, schools, and offices are closed, and different types of celebrations take place.

1. There is one national holiday celebrated in the United States.

   A. True
   B. False

2. A national holiday is recognized by:

   A. The federal government
   B. The state government
   C. The local government

3. Different types of celebrations take place across the country on national holidays.

   A. True
   B. False

4. Name another national holiday not listed above.

Yesterday you learned about national holidays. Today you will explore a special holiday in our country, Martin Luther King, Jr. Day.

Directions: Read the text below. Then answer the questions that follow.

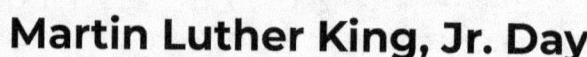

Martin Luther King, Jr. Day

Martin Luther King, Jr. Day is a national holiday that is celebrated on the third Monday of January every year. It is a celebration of Martin Luther King, Jr.'s birthday which was on January 15th. He was a very important civil rights activist who peacefully protested racial discrimination and unfair laws. Martin Luther King, Jr. was assassinated in 1968 at the age of 39. To honor him, celebrations take place in many cities across the country on his special day.

Directions: In the table below, write 3 important facts about Martin Luther King, Jr.

Fact #1	
Fact #2	
Fact #3	

Yesterday you learned about Martin Luther King, Jr. Day. Today you will explain why Veterans Day is an important national holiday.

Directions: Read the text below. Then answer the questions that follow.

Veterans Day is a national holiday celebrated on November 11th each year. It is a day to remember and honor all veterans. A **veteran** is a former member of the armed services or military. Many communities hold parades on Veterans Day.

1. Complete the sentence below.

Veterans Day is an important national holiday because

....

....

....

....

2. On the lines below, write two ways you could honor a veteran on Veterans Day.

....

....

....

....

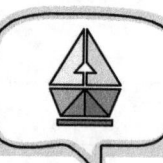
You have spent several days learning, exploring, and explaining important national holidays. Today you will write about ways you celebrate other national holidays.

Directions: On the table below, write things that your family does to celebrate each national holiday listed. You can also draw a picture in the box, if you choose.

New Year's Day	
Independence Day	
Thanksgiving Day	

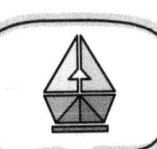

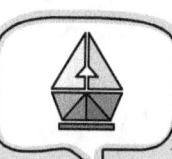
Yesterday you wrote about how your family celebrates certain national holidays. Today you will create your own national holiday and explain why it is important.

Directions: Think of a new national holiday. Then answer the questions below.

1. If you could create a new national holiday, what would it be?

....

....

....

....

....

2. When would it be celebrated?

....

....

....

....

....

3. Why would it be an important day to celebrate?

....

....

....

....

....

4. How would your family celebrate this new holiday?

....

....

....

....

....

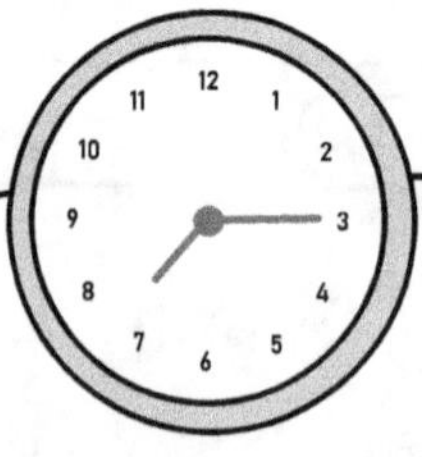

History

Timelines

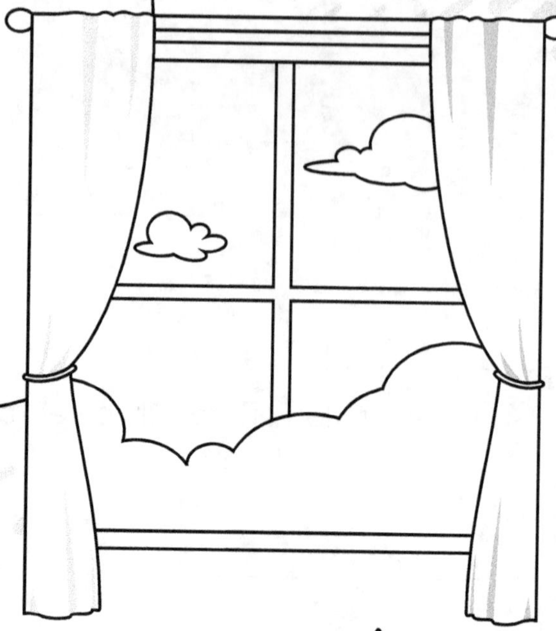

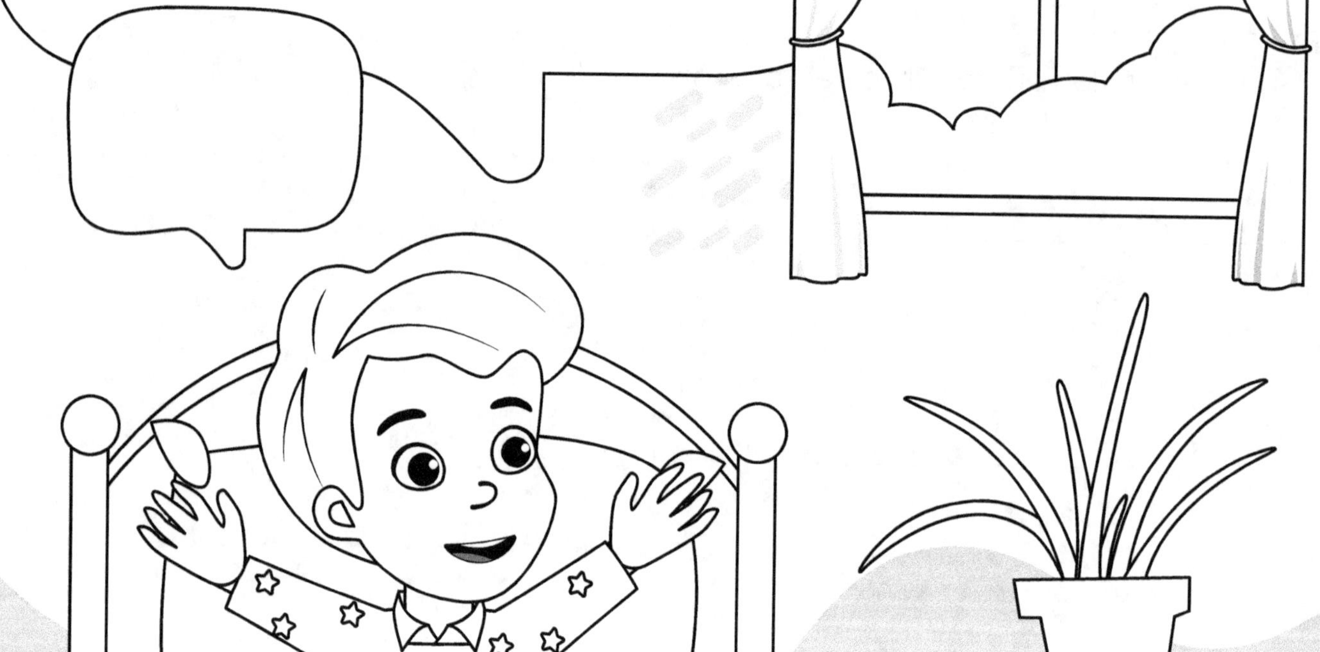

Develop a simple timeline of events in your life.

Directions: Read the text below. Then answer the questions that follow.

What is a Timeline?

A **timeline** is a graph of events in the order they happened. Timelines can be used to show important events from a person's life, historical events, or even the specific times when events happened. A timeline may be a small snapshot of time (the order of events at your last birthday party) or span many years (important events in your state's history over the last century). Timelines are great for showing a lot of information in an easy-to-read way.

1. Timelines only <u>sometimes</u> show events in chronological order, meaning ordered by time.

   A. True

   B. False

2. A timeline might be used to show:

   A. Events in history

   B. Important events in someone's life

   C. The order of your morning routine

   D. All of the above

3. Timelines can show very short or very long periods of time.

   A. True

   B. False

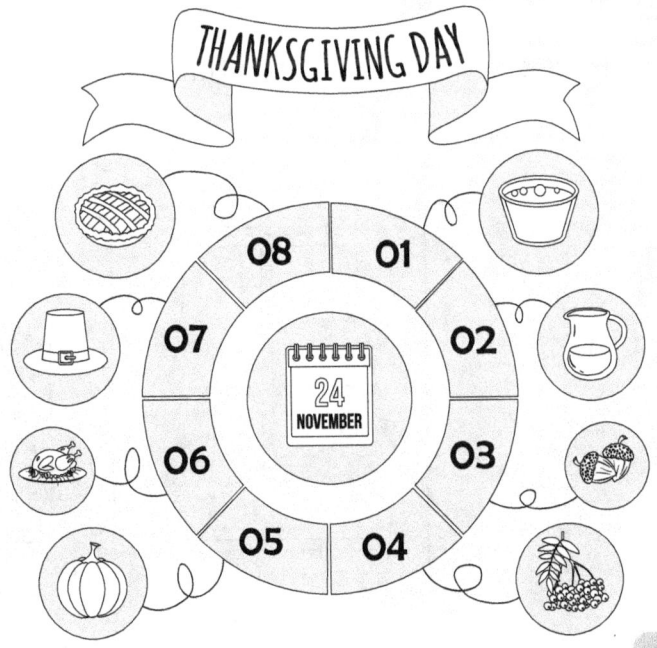

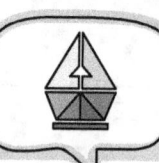
Yesterday you learned about timelines. Today you will explore a timeline of Jacob's morning routine.

Directions: Study the timeline below. Then answer the questions that follow.

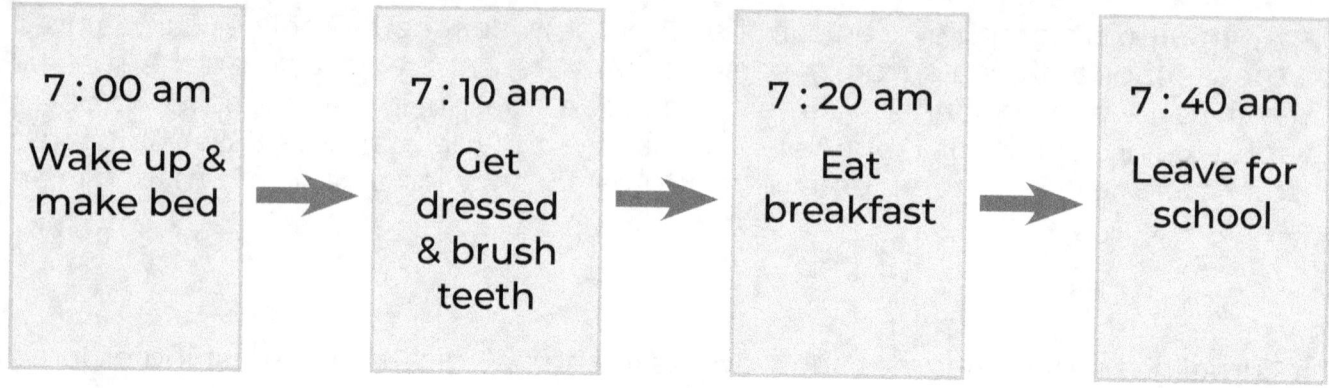

7:00 am — Wake up & make bed → 7:10 am — Get dressed & brush teeth → 7:20 am — Eat breakfast → 7:40 am — Leave for school

1. What time does Jacob eat breakfast each morning?

....

2. What does Jacob do right after he wakes up?

....

3. What does Jacob do right before he leaves for school?

....

4. Based on the timeline, what time does school possibly begin for Jacob?

....

5. Draw a picture of what Jacob does at 7:10 am.

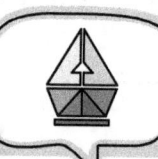
Yesterday you learned more about timelines. Today you will put events in order on a timeline and explain how you know where each piece should go.

Directions: Look at the timeline and events below. Decide where each event belongs on the timeline. Write the events in the correct box. Then answer the questions that follow.

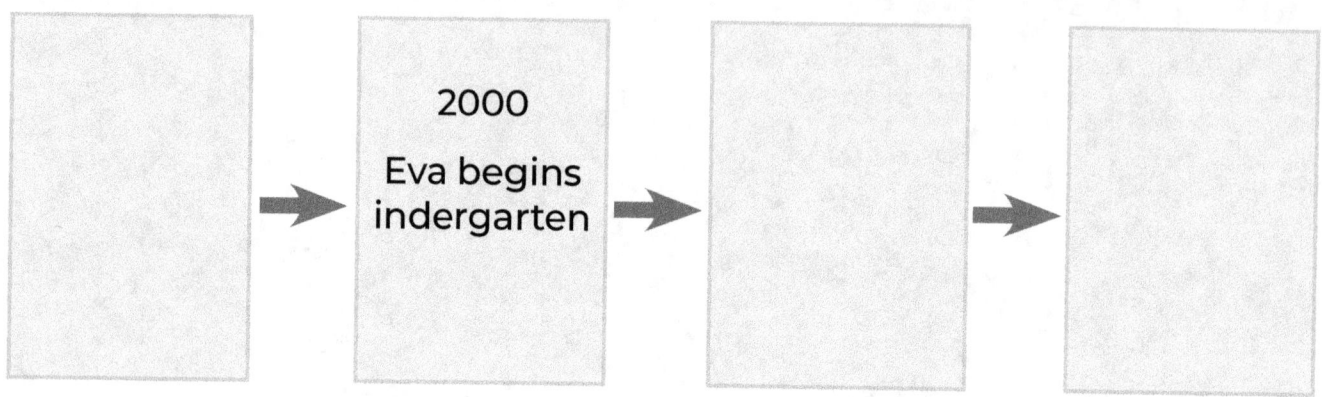

2000

Eva begins indergarten

2013	2020	1995
Eva graduates from high school.	Eva gets married.	Eva is born.

1. How did you know which order to put the events of Eva's life on the timeline?

_____

_____

_____

_____

_____

You have spent several days learning, exploring, and explaining how timelines work. Today you will create your own timeline of your life.

Directions: In the box below, create a timeline with important events from your own life. Be sure to include at least 5 events, and be sure the events are in chronological order.

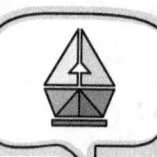
Yesterday you created a timeline of your own life. Today you will create a timeline of a character's life based on the passage below.

Directions: Read the passage below. Then use the information from the passage to create a timeline of the character's day.

Roberto woke up at 8:15 am last Tuesday. The sun was shining and the birds were chirping. He was so excited for the day because it was his birthday! He ran downstairs and saw several beautifully wrapped gifts on the table in the dining room. He couldn't wait to open them, but his parents were still asleep.

Finally, around 9:30 am, his parents and brother, Manuel, woke up and sat at the table. Roberto tore into his presents! He was so excited to open a brand new building block set. Ninety minutes later, he had the new set completely built!

At 11:30 am, many of Roberto's friends began to arrive for his birthday party. He was so excited to celebrate with them. About thirty minutes later, Roberto's mom called the boys down for his favorite lunch of pizza, potato chips, and cake.

By 1:00 pm, the boys had finished eating and were tired from playing outside. They came back into the house and Roberto opened more presents. His friends were so generous! He received so many great gifts that he was excited to play with! Roberto was so sad when 1:30 pm came and his friends had to leave. It was the best birthday party he'd ever had!

WEEK 5

History
American Folktales

Read and comprehend American folktales.

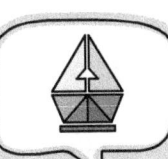
Directions: Read the text below. Then answer the questions that follow.

What is a Folktale?

A **folktale** is a fictional story that is told over and over again and passed down from one generation to the next. Folktales are usually told aloud and have no known author. Different folktales are told all over the world depending upon where you live. All folktales have some things in common. They teach a moral or lesson, have a problem and solution, and often include good versus evil.

1. Folktales are:

   A. Fiction

   B. Nonfiction

2. Different cultures have different folktales.

   A. True

   B. False

3. Which of the following is true about folktales? Circle all that apply.

   A. Folktales are written by a specific author.

   B. Folktales are usually told aloud rather than written down.

   C. Folktales usually teach us a lesson.

   D. Folktales always have animals as characters.

4. Folktales often have a moral. A moral is the same as:

   A. A character

   B. A setting

   C. A lesson

   D. A problem and solution

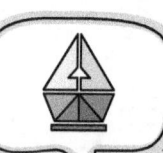
Yesterday you learned about folktales. Today you will explore the folktale, "The Boy Who Cried Wolf."

Directions: Read the folktale below. Then answer the questions that follow.

Once upon a time, there was a young boy who took care of sheep in a pasture far from town. Life in the pasture could get very boring. He entertained himself by using his imagination to make up stories.

One day, he wondered to himself what he would do if a wolf came along while he was tending the sheep. The townspeople always told him that he should call for help if he ever saw a wolf, and they would come help him. He decided to give it a try even though he had not seen a wolf. Very loudly, he began yelling, "Help! Wolf!"

Just as they promised, the townspeople stopped what they were doing to come and help the boy. When they arrived in the pasture, they did not find a wolf. Instead, they found the boy laughing and laughing at the trick he had played on them.

A few days later, the boy became bored again. Again, he began yelling, "Wolf! Wolf!" and once again, the townspeople ran to help him, only to find the boy laughing.

The next day, as the sun was setting over the pasture, a wolf leaped from behind some bushes. Frightened, the boy began yelling, "Help! Wolf!" Only this time, the townspeople did not believe the boy and refused to help him. Many of the boy's sheep were killed by the wolf, and the boy learned an important lesson.

Directions: Answer the questions that follow.

1. Circle the characters in the folktale.

2. Underline the setting(s) in the folktale.

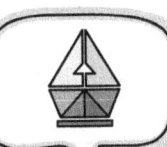
Yesterday you read the folktale, "The Boy Who Cried Wolf." Today you will explain the moral, or lesson, of the story.

Directions: Reread the folktale, "The Boy Who Cried Wolf," if necessary. Then complete the sentences below.

The moral, or lesson, of the folktale is

....

....

....

....

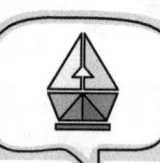
I know this is the moral of the folktale because

....

....

....

....

....

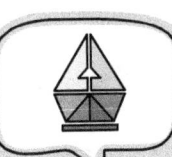
You have spent several days learning, exploring, and explaining what a folktale is. Today, you will read another folktale, "The Tortoise and the Hare."

Directions: Read the folktale below. Then answer the questions that follow.

One day, Hare was making fun of Tortoise for being so slow. As Hare laughed at him, Tortoise replied, "I can get places sooner than you think, and I'll prove it by racing you." This amused Hare, but he agreed to it.

The next day, Fox, the judge of the race, started them off. Hare was quickly far out of sight. To show Tortoise how ridiculous it was that he challenged him to a race, Hare decided to lay down and take a nap.

Meanwhile, Tortoise kept moving slowly but steadily. Soon, he passed the place where Hare slept peacefully. Tortoise continued on, being sure to not wake Hare. When Hare finally awoke, Tortoise was almost across the finish line. Hare ran as quickly as he could to catch up to Tortoise, but he could not. Tortoise crossed the finish line first and won the race.

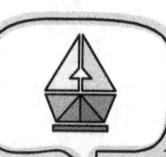
Directions: Complete the sentence below.

The moral, or lesson, of the folktale is

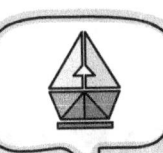
Yesterday you analyzed another folktale. Today you will make a connection between the folktale, "The Tortoise and the Hare" and your own life.

Directions: Reread the folktale, "The Tortoise and the Hare," if necessary. Think of a time you felt like either Tortoise or Hare. Complete the sentence below. Then draw a picture that matches your sentence.

I felt like ....

when ....

....

....

WEEK 6

Civics and Government

Rights and Responsibilities

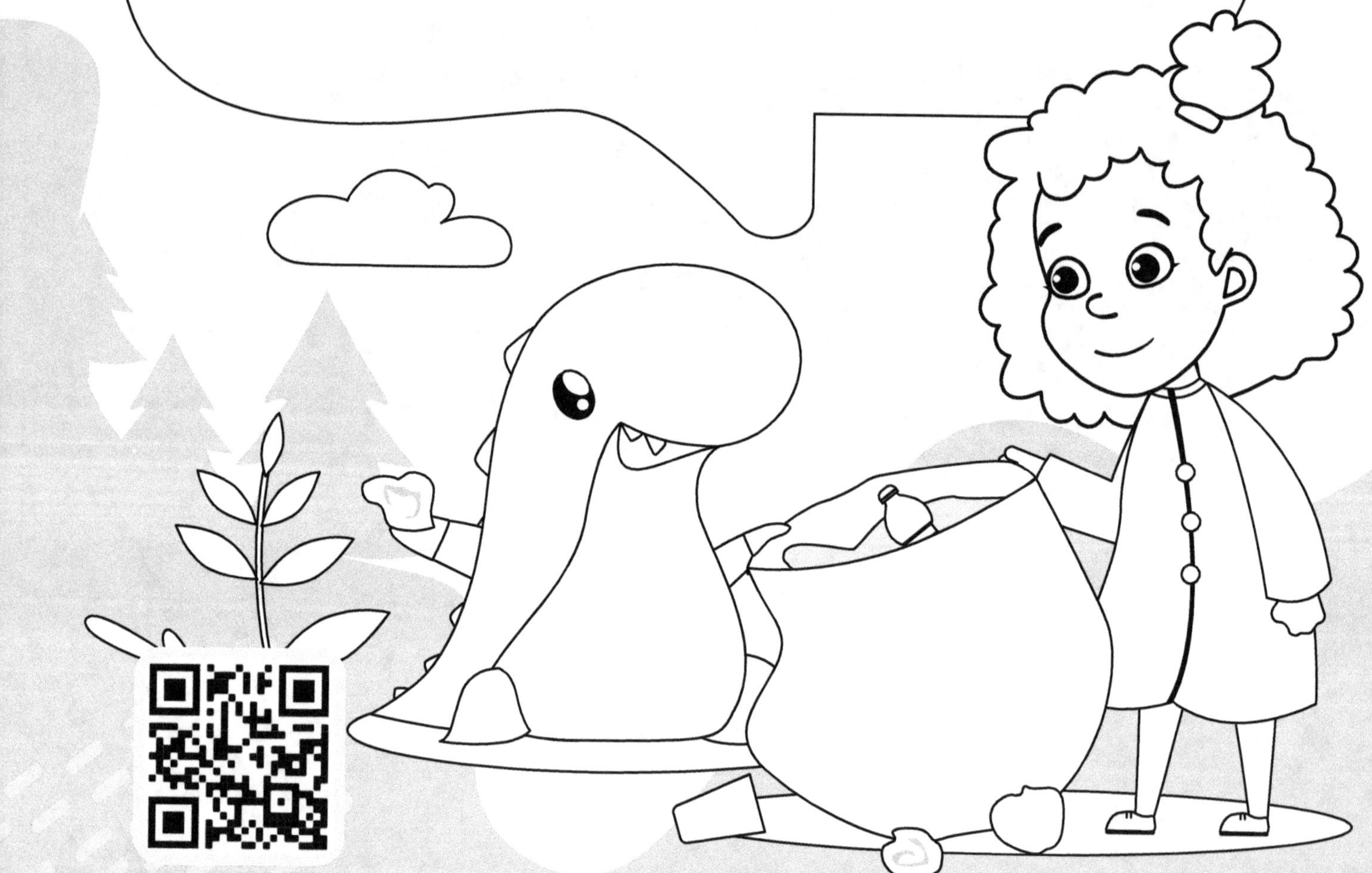

Understand and explain the difference between rights and responsibilities.

Directions: Read the text below. Then answer the questions that follow.

Rights and Responsibilities

Citizens of the United States have many rights and responsibilities. A **right** is something people are entitled to or deserve. For instance, in our country, we have the right to receive a free education. We also have the right to practice whichever religion we choose. A **responsibility** is something people are expected to do or take care of. We have many responsibilities as citizens, such as caring for our neighbors and following the rules and laws.

1. Rights are:

    A. Something people deserve

    B. Something people are expected to do

2. Responsibilities are:

    A. Something people deserve

    B. Something people are expected to do

3. Which of the following are rights? Circle all that apply.

    A. Freedom of speech

    B. Freedom of religion

    C. Jobs

    D. Education

4. Rights and responsibilities are both important to citizens.

    A. True

    B. False

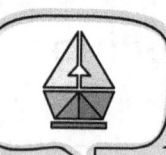
Yesterday you learned about rights and responsibilities. Today you will explore these concepts further.

Directions: Read the table below that lists the rights and responsibilities of students at school. Then answer the questions that follow.

Students have the right to:	Students are responsible for:
• Feel safe at school • Voice their own thoughts and ideas • Be respected • Be listened to • Be treated fairly • Be themselves	• Completing their work • Making positive choices • Respecting others • Treating others fairly • Being cooperative • Listening to others

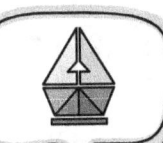
Directions: Answer the questions that follow.

1. Which of the following belongs in the RIGHTS column on the table? Circle all that apply.

   A. Be respectful of others' belongings

   B. Make choices about their learning

   C. Learn new things

   D. Help keep a safe environment in the classroom

2. Which of the following belongs in the RESPONSIBILITIES column on the table? Circle all that apply.

   A. Be respectful of others' belongings

   B. Make choices about their learning

   C. Learn new things

   D. Help keep a safe environment in the classroom

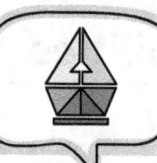
Yesterday you learned more about the rights and responsibilities of students at school. Today you will explain whether something is a right or a responsibility and why.

Directions: Read each phrase below. Decide whether it is a right or a responsibility. Circle the correct answer. Then, explain your thinking.

1. To follow the rules

   A. Right

   B. Responsibility

   Explanation: _____

   _____

2. To be safe

   A. Right

   B. Responsibility

   Explanation: _____

   _____

   _____

   _____

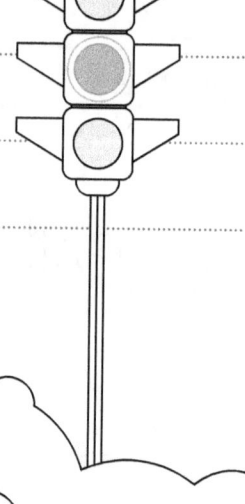

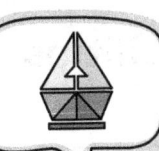
3. To clean up after ourselves

   A. Right

   B. Responsibility

Explanation: ....

....

....

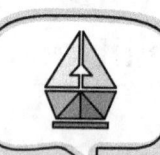
You have spent several days learning, exploring, and explaining the difference between rights and responsibilities. Today, you will decide which responsibilities go along with the rights you have at home.

Directions: Read each of the rights below. Then list at least one responsibility that goes along with having that right.

1. You have the right to shelter, or a home to live in.

What is a responsibility that goes along with having a home?

....

....

2. You have the right to be fed at breakfast, lunch and dinner.

What is a responsibility that goes along with having food to eat?

....

....

3. You have the right to have clothing to wear.

What is a responsibility that goes along with having your own clothing?

....

....

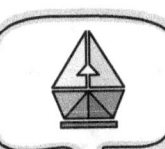
Yesterday you listed responsibilities that go along with the rights you have at home. Today you will come up with your own right and responsibility combination.

Directions: Complete the sentences below.

I have the right to:

....

....

....

Because I have this right, I am responsible for:

....

....

....

....

WEEK 7

Civics and Government

Rules and Laws

Define and give examples of rules and laws in the school and community.

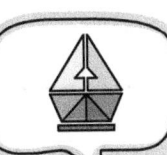
Directions: Read the text below. Then answer the questions that follow.

Rules and Laws

There are many rules and laws that we must follow. A **rule** is something you follow in order to keep yourself and others safe in certain places. There are rules at home and at school. A **law** is a rule that everyone in a community must obey, or follow. Laws are created by the government and protect us. Cities, states, and countries have laws. There are consequences for breaking rules or laws.

1. Rules are:

   A. Something you follow in a certain place to keep people safe

   B. Something that must be obeyed by everyone in a community

2. Laws are:

   A. Something you follow in a certain place to keep people safe

   B. Something that must be obeyed by everyone in a community

3. Where might there be rules to follow? Circle <u>all</u> that apply.

   A. School

   B. Home

   C. Library

   D. Park

4. Both rules and laws are meant to keep us safe.

   A. True

   B. False

Yesterday you learned about rules and laws. Today you will explore these concepts further.

Directions: Read the table below that lists different rules and laws. Then answer the questions that follow.

School Rules:	State Laws:
• Walk quietly in the hallways	• Obey the speed limit
• Raise your hand before speaking	• Wear your seatbelt
• Listen when others are speaking	• Don't text while driving

Directions: Answer the questions that follow.

1. Which of the following belong in the RULES column on the table? Circle all that apply.

   A. Be respectful of others' belongings

   B. Ask to use the restroom

   C. Talk to others in the cafeteria

   D. Clean up after yourself in the cafeteria

2. Which of the following belong in the LAWS column on the table? Circle all that apply.

   A. Help keep a safe environment in the classroom

   B. Throw your trash away at the park

   C. Be kind to others at the pool

   D. Stop at a red light

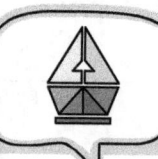
Yesterday you learned more about rules and laws. Today you will decide whether something is a rule or a law.

Directions: Read each phrase on the next page. Decide whether it is a rule or a law. Write the phrases in the correct place on the table.

Rule	Law

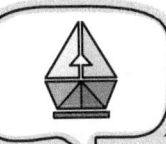
Raise your hand for permission to speak	Stop your car at all stop signs	Do not throw trash on the ground
Walk in a single file line in the hallway	Complete homework before playtime	Do not take items from a store without paying for them first

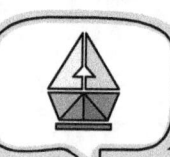
You have spent several days learning, exploring, and explaining the difference between rules and laws. Today you will make a list of rules you have at home.

Directions: What rules do you have at home? Make a list in the table below.

Your Rules at Home

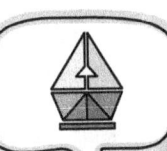
Yesterday you listed rules you have at home. Today you will explain why rules and laws are important.

Directions: Complete the sentence below. Then draw a picture to match your sentence.

Rules and laws are important because:

....

....

WEEK 8

Civics and Government

The Common Good

Describe ways the actions of individuals can contribute to the common good of a classroom or community.

ARGOPREP

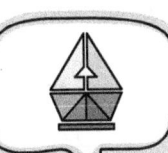
Directions: Read the text below. Then answer the questions that follow.

What are the Responsibilities of Citizens?

Citizens, or members of a community, are responsible for many things. They must follow the rules and laws to keep everyone safe. It is also important that citizens contribute to the **common good** of their community. To contribute to the common good means to do things for the benefit of all people in the community, not just for themselves. For example, a student who donates pencils to his teacher for classroom use is contributing to the common good of the classroom. The student has done something that will benefit every student in the classroom.

1. Citizens are responsible for:

   A. Following rules and laws

   B. Contributing to the common good

   C. Both a and b

2. To contribute to the common good means to do something for:

   A. Yourself

   B. Someone else

   C. All members of the community

3. Which might be an example of contributing to the common good? Circle all that apply.

   A. Bringing a snack for yourself to enjoy during snack time at school

   B. Bringing a snack for you and your best friend to enjoy during snack time at school

   C. Bringing a snack to share with all your classmates during snack time at school

   D. Donating snacks to your teacher for classmates to enjoy during snack time at school

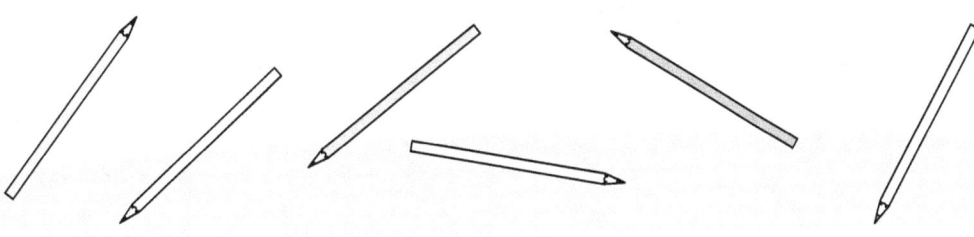

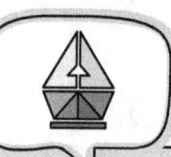
Yesterday you learned about contributing to the common good. Today you will explore this concept further.

Directions: Read the table below that lists different examples of actions done by students in a school. Decide if the action is an example of contributing to the common good or not. Write yes or no on the right-hand side of the table.

Is this an example of contributing to the common good?	Yes or No
1. Juan cleaned up the whole table he sat at for lunch.	1.
2. Bo brought a birthday present for his friend, Max.	2.
3. Oliver shared his eraser with a classmate who sits next to him during writing time.	3.
4. Rosalee and Ruby picked up trash on the playground during their recess time.	4.
5. Bryan and his mom helped raise money for new soccer balls for the gym teacher.	5.
6. Ms. Davis gave Aaron a new pair of socks.	6.

Yesterday you decided whether or not certain actions were contributing to the common good. Today you will choose one of those actions to explain.

Directions: Choose an action from yesterday's list that WAS an example of contributing to the common good. Complete the sentence below.

Action:

....

....

....

This action was an example of contributing to the common good because:

....

....

....

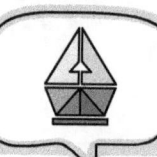
You have spent several days learning, exploring, and explaining actions that are examples of contributing to the common good. Today you will create your own example and non-example of actions that contribute to the common good.

Directions: On the lines below, write an example of an action you could take that contributes to the common good of your classroom, school, or local community.

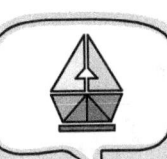
Directions: On the lines below, write an example of an action you could take that is **NOT** contributing to the common good of your classroom, school, or local community.

....

....

....

....

....

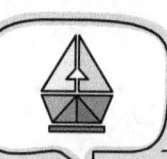
Yesterday you listed an example and non-example of actions that contribute to the common good. Today you will explain why contributing to the common good is important.

Directions: Complete the sentence below. Then draw a picture to match your sentence.

Contributing to the common good is important because:

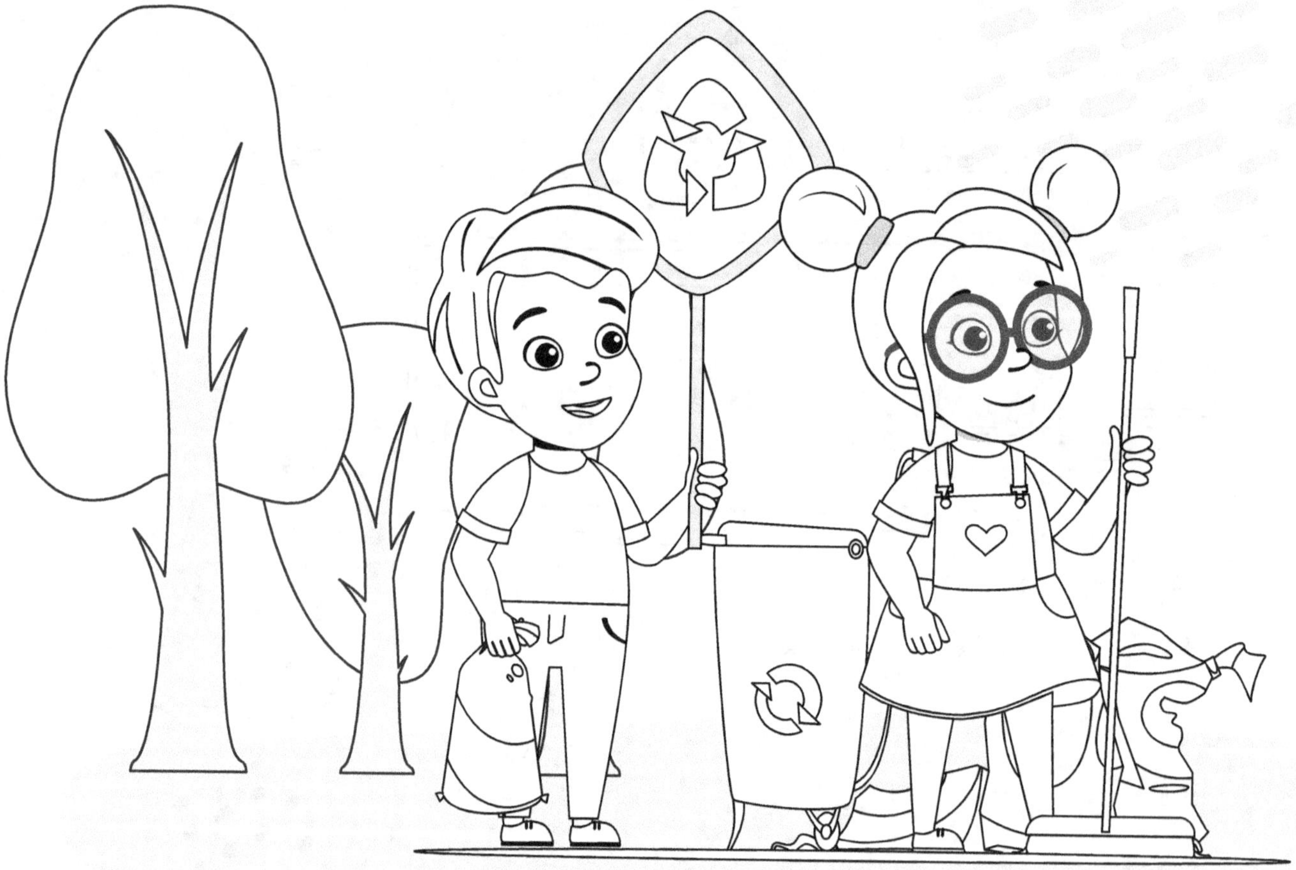

....

....

....

....

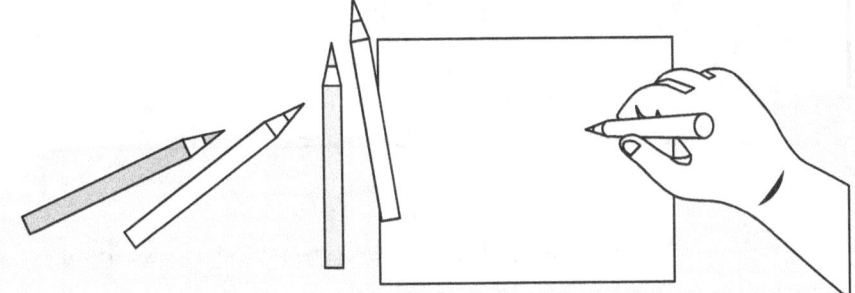

Civics and Government

Being a Good Citizen

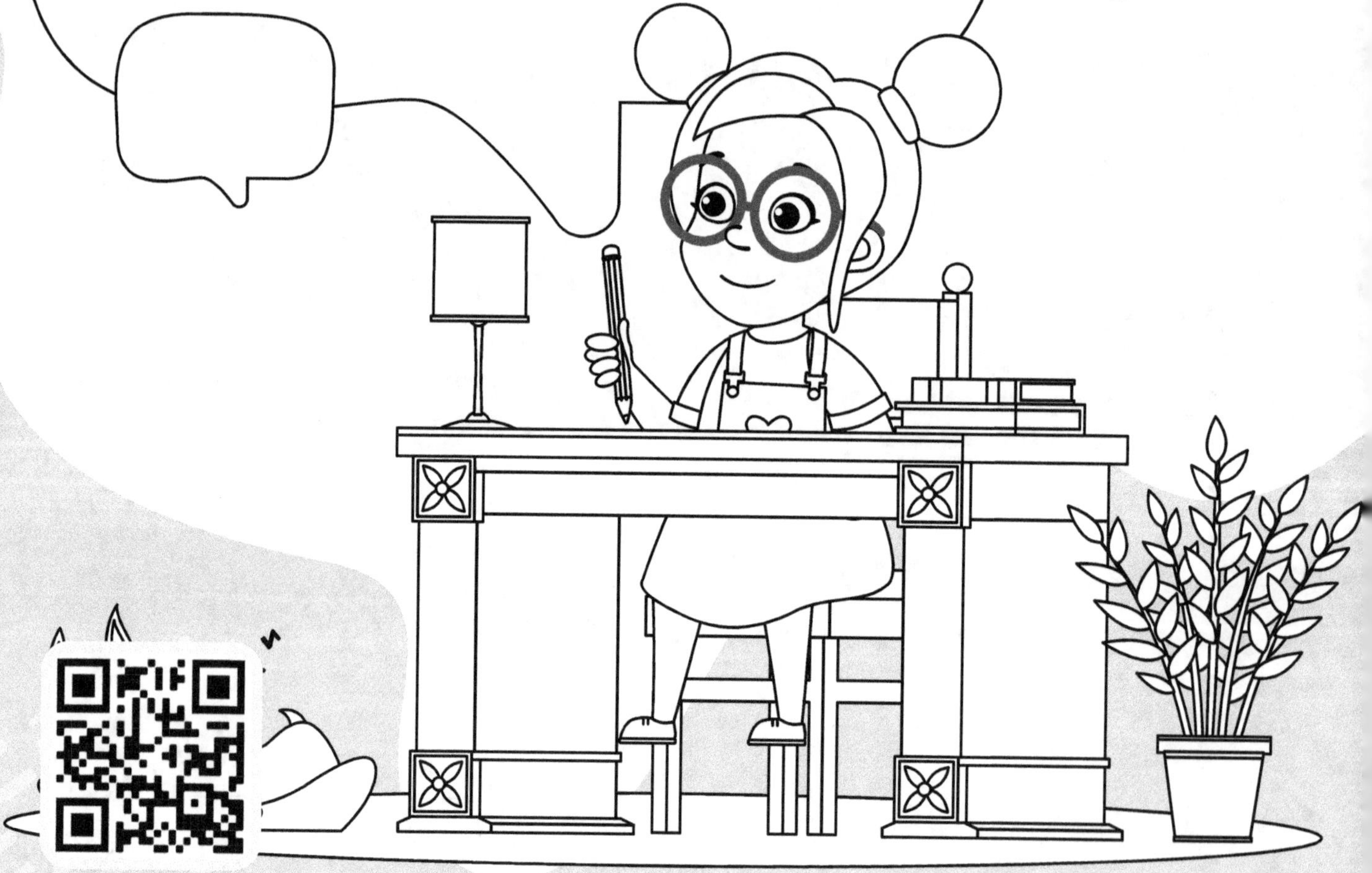

Describe what it means to be a good citizen.

Directions: Read the text below. Then answer the questions that follow.

What Does it Mean to be a Good Citizen?

Citizens are members of a community such as a school, city, or country. Being a good citizen means helping take care of the community and the people who are part of it. You can do this by being respectful of others in the community. You can help others when they need it, clean up shared spaces, and follow the rules and laws.

1. You can be a citizen of:

   A. A school

   B. A neighborhood

   C. A city

   D. A state

   E. All of the above

2. Being a good citizen is not important.

   A. True

   B. False

3. Which might be an example of being a good citizen? Circle all that apply.

   A. Cleaning up after having a picnic at the park

   B. Not sharing your eraser with a classmate at school

   C. Helping an elderly neighbor carry groceries into their house

   D. Greeting the mailman by name

   E. Shouting out answers during circle time at school

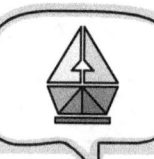
Yesterday you learned what it means to be a good citizen. Today you will explore this concept further.

Directions: Read the scenario below. Then answer the questions that follow.

> Today is Julio's first day at his new school. His dad just got a new job, so his family moved from New York to Texas. Julio is very nervous about making new friends at school.
>
> When he is taken to his new classroom, his teacher, Mrs. Barnes, asks Cody to help Julio get around during his first week at school. Cody is kind and agrees to help Julio.
>
> Throughout the day, whenever the class leaves to go somewhere else, Cody stays by Julio's side and makes sure he knows where he is going. Cody also introduces Julio to many of his friends, as well as other teachers at the school.
>
> At the end of the first day, Julio is getting his backpack ready to go home. Cody comes over and offers to walk home with Julio. Julio can't believe he had such a great first day at school and has even made a new friend!

1. In the text, Cody is an example of a:

   A. Good citizen

   B. Bad citizen

2. List 3 characteristics that describe Cody.

   A. ....

   B. ....

   C. ....

Yesterday you decided whether or not a character in a passage displayed the characteristics of a good citizen. Today you will use the text to give examples of these characteristics.

Directions: Answer the questions below.

1. Give 3 examples of good citizenship from yesterday's text.

   A. _____

   _____

   B. _____

   _____

   C. _____

   _____

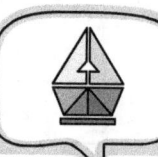
2. Choose one of the characteristics you listed above to explain below. Complete the sentence.

Cody showed

when he

You have spent several days learning, exploring, and explaining actions that are examples of good citizenship. Today you will write about a time that you showed good citizenship and a time when you did not.

Directions: On the lines below, write an example of a time you showed good citizenship in your classroom, school, or local community.

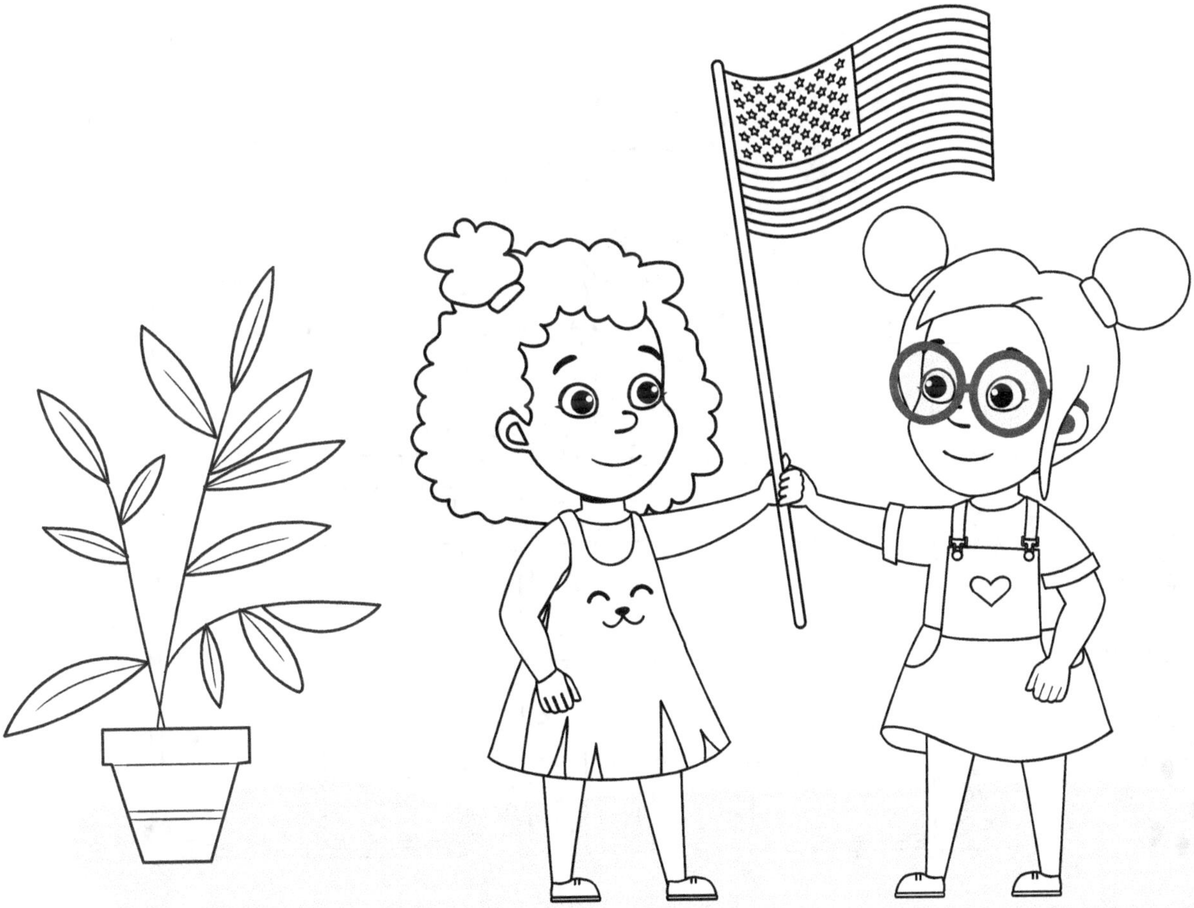

....

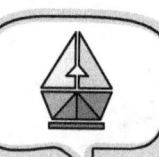
Directions: On the lines below, write an example of a time you did **NOT** show good citizenship in your classroom, school, or local community.

....

....

....

....

....

....

Yesterday you wrote about a time you showed good citizenship and a time you did not. Today you will draw a picture that shows what good citizenship might look like.

Directions: Draw a picture that shows what good citizenship might look like.

Civics and Government

The Pledge of Allegiance

Recite the Pledge of Allegiance and understand its meaning.

ARGOPREP

Directions: Read the text below. Then answer the questions that follow.

The Pledge of Allegiance

The Pledge of Allegiance was written by a minister in 1892. He wrote it when schools around the United States were preparing to celebrate the 400th anniversary of Columbus Day. The words were slightly changed in 1924 and again in 1954. Today, many schools around the country still recite The Pledge of Allegiance together every morning.

1. The Pledge of Allegiance has never been changed since it was written in 1892.

   A. True
   B. False

2. The Pledge of Allegiance was written by:

   A. A teacher
   B. A principal
   C. A minister
   D. An author

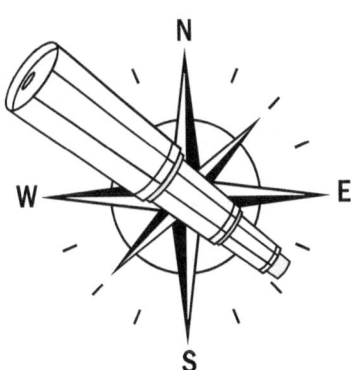

3. The Pledge of Allegiance was written for what purpose?

   A. To honor the American flag
   B. To give school children something to recite each day
   C. To honor the President
   D. To help celebrate the anniversary of Columbus Day

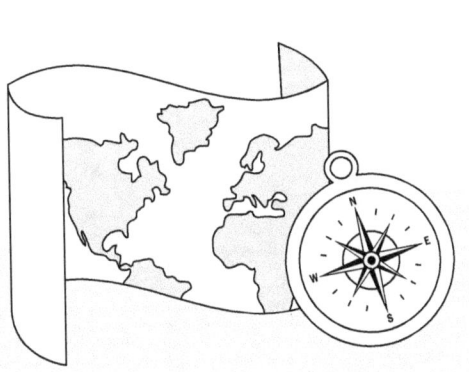

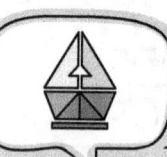

Yesterday you learned about The Pledge of Allegiance. Today you will explore the words in The Pledge.

I pledge allegiance to the flag of the United States of America, and to the Republic for which it stands, one nation under God, indivisible, with liberty and justice for all.

Directions: Read the words in the left hand column of the table below. Then read the definitions on the next page. Match each definition with the correct word. Write the corresponding letter in the right hand column of the table.

1. allegiance	
2. nation	
3. indivisible	
4. liberty	
5. justice	

A. Freedom

B. Loyalty to the government

C. Fair or right

D. Impossible to divide or separate

E. Country

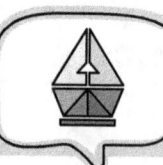
Yesterday you learned what the words in The Pledge of Allegiance mean. Today you will explain what you think The Pledge of Allegiance means.

Directions: Reread the words in The Pledge of Allegiance from yesterday. Complete the sentence below.

I think The Pledge of Allegiance means

....

....

....

because

....

....

....

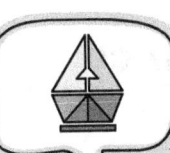
You have spent several days learning, exploring, and explaining the words in The Pledge of Allegiance. Today you will write about your experience reciting The Pledge of Allegiance.

Directions: On the lines below, write about how The Pledge of Allegiance is recited at your school. Then draw a picture to match your sentence.

Yesterday you wrote about how The Pledge of Allegiance is recited at your school. Today you will practice reciting The Pledge of Allegiance.

Directions: Read The Pledge of Allegiance below. Some of the words are missing. Fill in the missing words by writing them on the line provided.

.... **pledge allegiance** .... **the flag**

.... **the United States of America**
.... **to**

the Republic .... **which** .... **stands,**

.... **nation under God, indivisible,**
....

liberty .... **justice for** ....**.**

WEEK 11

Geography
Cardinal Directions

Identify the cardinal directions (north, east, south and west) on maps and globes and within the classroom or school.

ARGOPREP

Directions: Read the text below. Then answer the questions that follow.

Cardinal Directions

Cardinal directions are the four main points on a compass - north, east, south and west. They can be found on maps and globes. Sometimes cardinal directions are abbreviated, or shortened, to the letters: N, E, S, and W. Cardinal directions are useful in helping people get from one point to another.

1. There are 8 cardinal directions.

    A. True

    B. False

2. Cardinal directions are useful to people when they are traveling.

    A. True

    B. False

3. Which of the following is NOT a cardinal direction?

    A. West

    B. Southeast

    C. North

    D. South

4. Where might you find cardinal directions?

    A. Globe

    B. Compass

    C. Map

    D. All of the above

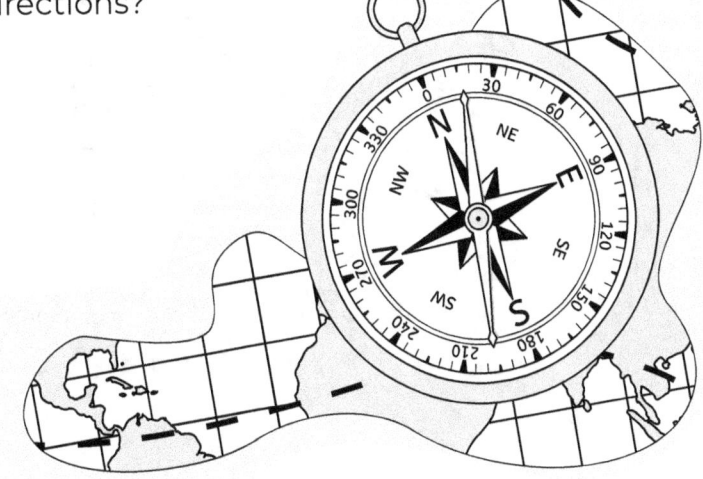

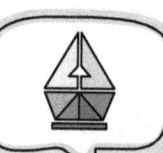
Yesterday you learned about cardinal directions. Today you will learn about the difference between a compass and a compass rose.

Directions: Read the text below. Then answer the questions that follow.

A **compass** is a tool that helps you find directions. It has a magnetic needle inside that can spin in circles, but the needle always points north. A **compass rose** is slightly different from a compass. It is a drawing that is found on maps to show different directions.

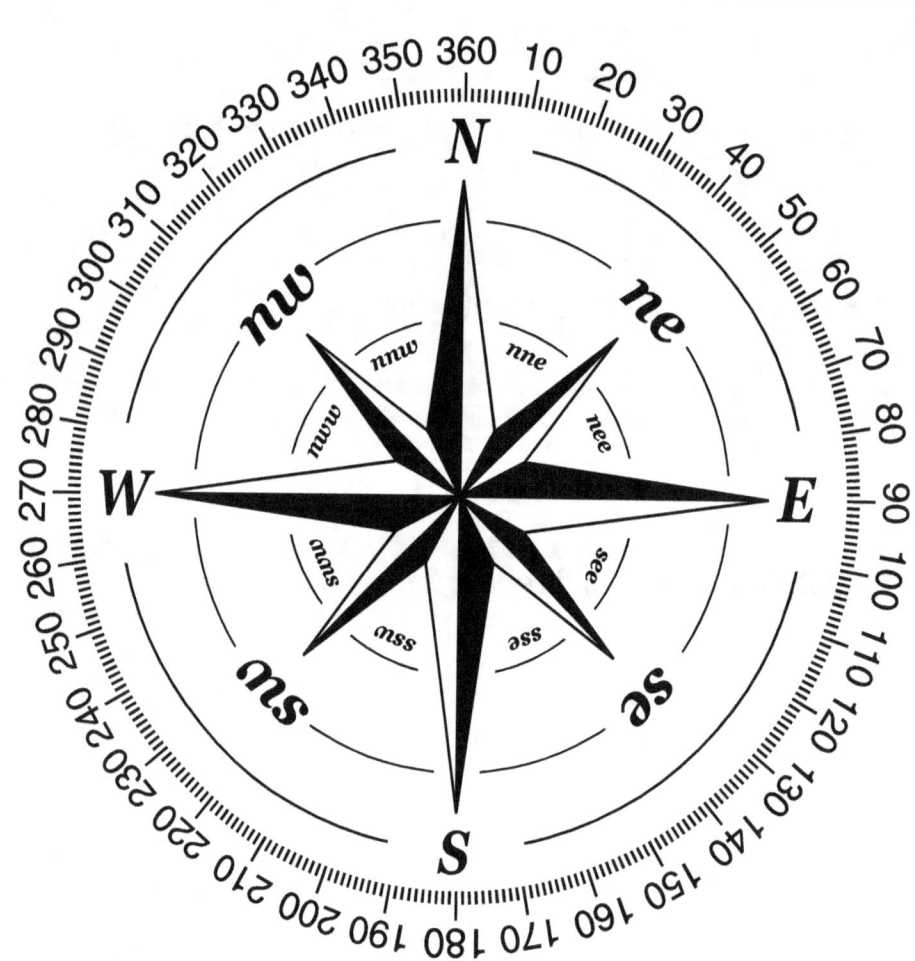

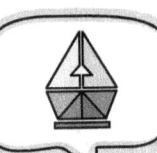
Directions: Read each scenario below. Decide if a compass or compass rose would be most useful. Write your answer on the line.

1. Juanita is looking at a map and trying to figure out which state is north of the state she lives in. Would a compass or compass rose be most helpful?

....

....

....

2. Mike and his friend are hiking in the woods. They need to head south to get back to their car. Would a compass or compass rose be most helpful?

....

....

....

3. Rose is planning a road trip. She is using a map to plan her route, and she needs to know which highway heads west. Would a compass or compass rose be most helpful?

....

....

....

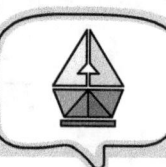
Yesterday you learned the difference between a compass and a compass rose. Today you will write about a time that each tool might be helpful.

Directions: Reread the scenarios from yesterday. Write your own scenario describing a time that each tool might be helpful.

1. Compass

....

....

....

....

2. Compass rose

....

....

....

....

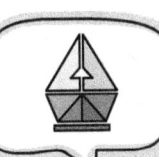
You have spent several days learning, exploring, and explaining cardinal directions. Today you will use the compass rose below to show the direction of places in your neighborhood.

Directions: Label the four cardinal directions on the compass rose below. Then write one thing that can be found in each direction of your house. For instance, what place can be found to the north, east, south, or west of your house?

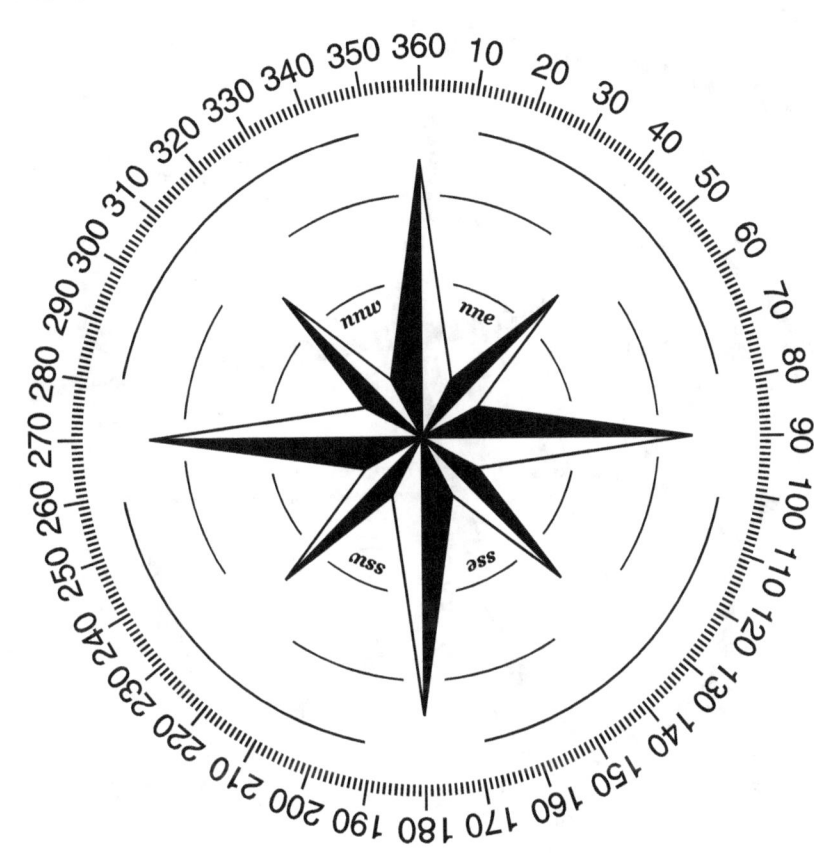

1. North: ....

2. East : ....

3. South: ....

4. West: ....

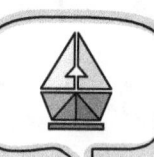
Yesterday you labeled a compass rose and identified places around your neighborhood. Today you will practice using cardinal directions.

Directions: Use the map of the city below to answer the questions.

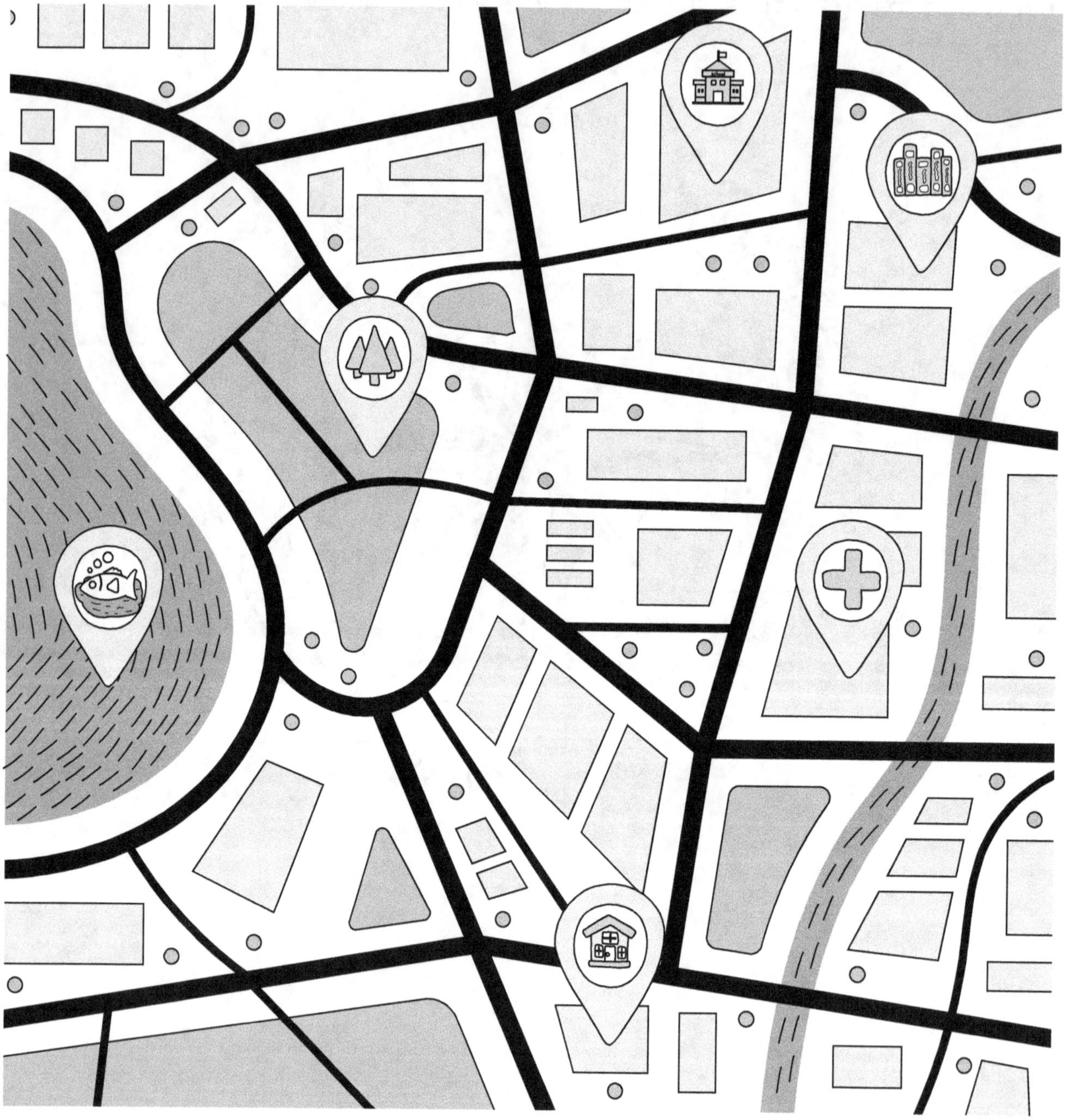

1. The library is .... of the school.

2. The park is .... of the hospital.

3. The pond is .... of the library.

4. What can be found west of the hospital?

....

....

....

5. What can be found south of the school?

....

....

....

6. List two things that are east of the pond.

....

....

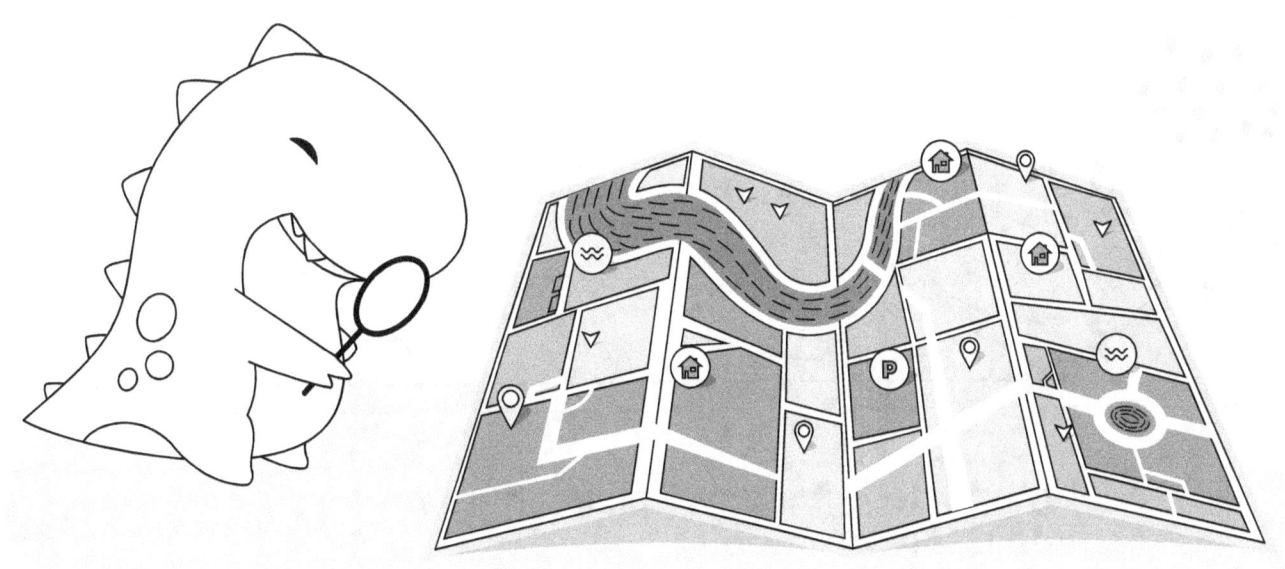

WEEK 12

Geography

Physical vs. Human Features

Identify and describe physical and human features in the community.

ARGOPREP

Directions: Read the text below. Then answer the questions that follow.

Physical Features vs. Human Features - What's the Difference?

Our world is full of both physical and human features. **Physical features** are things that are found in nature such as landforms, bodies of water, plants, and animals. Mountains, oceans, trees, and birds are all examples of physical features. **Human features** are things that are man-made, or created by humans. This includes things such as buildings, cities, roads, and farms. All of these physical and human features come together to make up our world!

1. Physical and human features are the same thing.

   A. True
   B. False

2. The Atlantic Ocean is an example of a:

   A. Physical feature
   B. Human feature

3. The Empire State Building is an example of a:

   A. Physical feature
   B. Human feature

4. Physical features:

   A. Are made by humans
   B. Are created with building materials
   C. Happen naturally

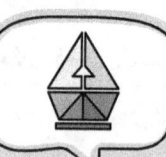
Yesterday you learned about physical and human features. Today you will explore examples of each.

Directions: Read the text below. Then answer the questions that follow.

Physical features are things that are found in nature. They happen naturally. **Human features** are things that are man-made, or created by humans.

Directions: Read each feature below. Decide if it is a physical feature or human feature. Write your answer on the line.

1. Mediterranean Sea

....

....

2. The Smoky Mountains

....

....

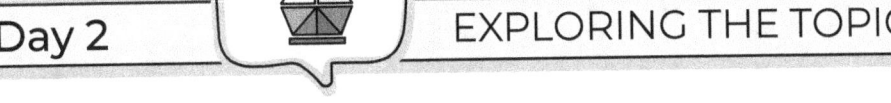
3. A skyscraper

....

....

4. The Nile River

....

....

5. The homes in your neighborhood

....

....

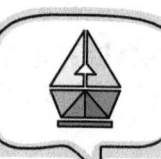
Yesterday you learned more about physical and human features. Today you will write about the difference between the two.

Directions: Read and complete the sentences below to make them true.

1. A physical feature is made by ....

....

2. An example of a physical feature is ....

....

....

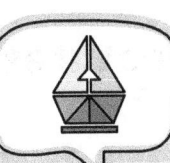
3. A human feature is made by ....

....

....

4. An example of a human feature is ....

....

....

....

5. The main difference between physical and human features is ....

....

....

....

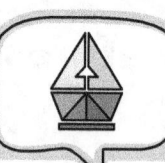
You have spent several days learning, exploring, and explaining the differences between physical and human features. Today you will create a picture of your own neighborhood and label the physical and human features.

Directions: Draw a picture in the box below of your neighborhood. Label each of the physical and human features in your drawing.

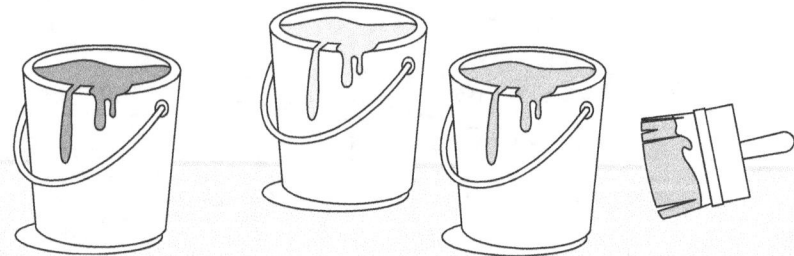

Week 12
Day 5

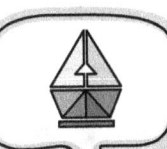

Physical vs. Human Features
ELABORATING ON THE TOPIC

Yesterday you labeled a drawing of your own neighborhood. Today you will make a list of all the physical and human features you can think of.

Directions: Use the table below to write your answers.

Physical Features	Human Features

Geography

Weather

Summarize weather patterns in different communities.

ARGOPREP

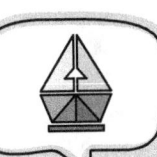
Directions: Read the text below. Then answer the questions that follow.

Weather Patterns

Different areas of the United States have different weather patterns. A **weather pattern** is when the weather repeats itself at different times of the year. For instance, depending on where you live, each season will probably have a similar type of weather. Maybe summers are always very hot, and winters are always very snowy. These are weather patterns. The different seasons happen at different times of the year depending on your location on the Earth.

1. Weather patterns are the same all over the United States.

   A. True

   B. False

2. In the winter, some areas of the United States are warm while others are cold.

   A. True

   B. False

3. Weather patterns are determined by: (Circle all that apply.)

   A. The season

   B. Your location

   C. Holidays

   D. People's moods

4. What is the weather like in winter where you live?

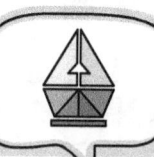
Yesterday you learned about weather patterns. Today you will learn more about the different aspects of weather.

Directions: Read the text below. Then answer the questions that follow.

What is Weather?

Weather patterns are made up of temperature (how hot or cold it is), precipitation (rainfall and snowfall), cloud cover, and amount of sunlight. The four seasons (winter, spring, summer and fall) depend on the time of year and the location on Earth. In winter, the days are shorter with less sunlight, and in summer, the days are longer with more sunlight.

Directions: Read each sentence below. Complete the sentence with the correct answer.

1. Weather patterns are made up of .... ,

.... , ... and

....

2. The four seasons are .... , ... ,

.... and ....

3. In winter, the days are .... and the nights are

....

4. In summer, the days are .... and the nights are

....

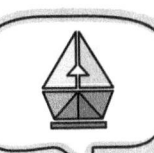
Yesterday you learned more about weather patterns. Today you will summarize the weather pattern after reading a short paragraph.

Directions: Read the text below. Then answer the questions that follow.

Lisa lives in Michigan. In the winter, she likes to ski, snowboard, and have snowball fights with her friends. Once it begins to warm up in the springtime, Lisa likes to play at the park and plant the garden with her mom. After school gets out, Lisa's favorite summertime activity is going to the beach to swim. The lake is one of her favorite places! In fall, lots of farmers in Michigan grow delicious apples. Lisa and her dad often drive to the apple orchard on the weekend to pick fresh, juicy apples to eat. Usually, the apple orchards have other things for kids to do like playgrounds and corn mazes.

Directions: Summarize the weather patterns in Michigan, based on the text. What do you think the weather is like during each season?

1. In winter, the weather is probably:

....

....

....

2. In spring, the weather is probably:

....

....

....

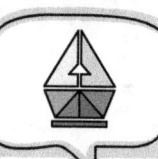

3. In summer, the weather is probably:

....

....

....

....

4. In fall, the weather is probably:

....

....

....

....

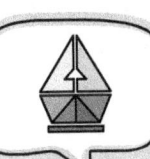
You have spent several days learning, exploring, and explaining weather patterns. Today you will write a summary of the weather patterns where you live.

Directions: Using yesterday's activity as an example, write a summary of the weather patterns where you live on the lines below.

Winter: ....

....

....

....

Spring: ....

....

....

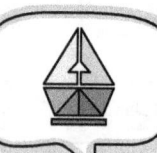
Summer: ....

....

....

....

....

Fall: ....

....

....

....

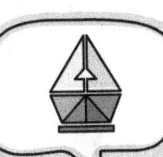
Yesterday you summarized the weather patterns for your hometown. Today you will draw pictures to match your summary for each season.

Directions: Draw a picture of each season where you live below.

Winter	Spring
Summer	**Fall**

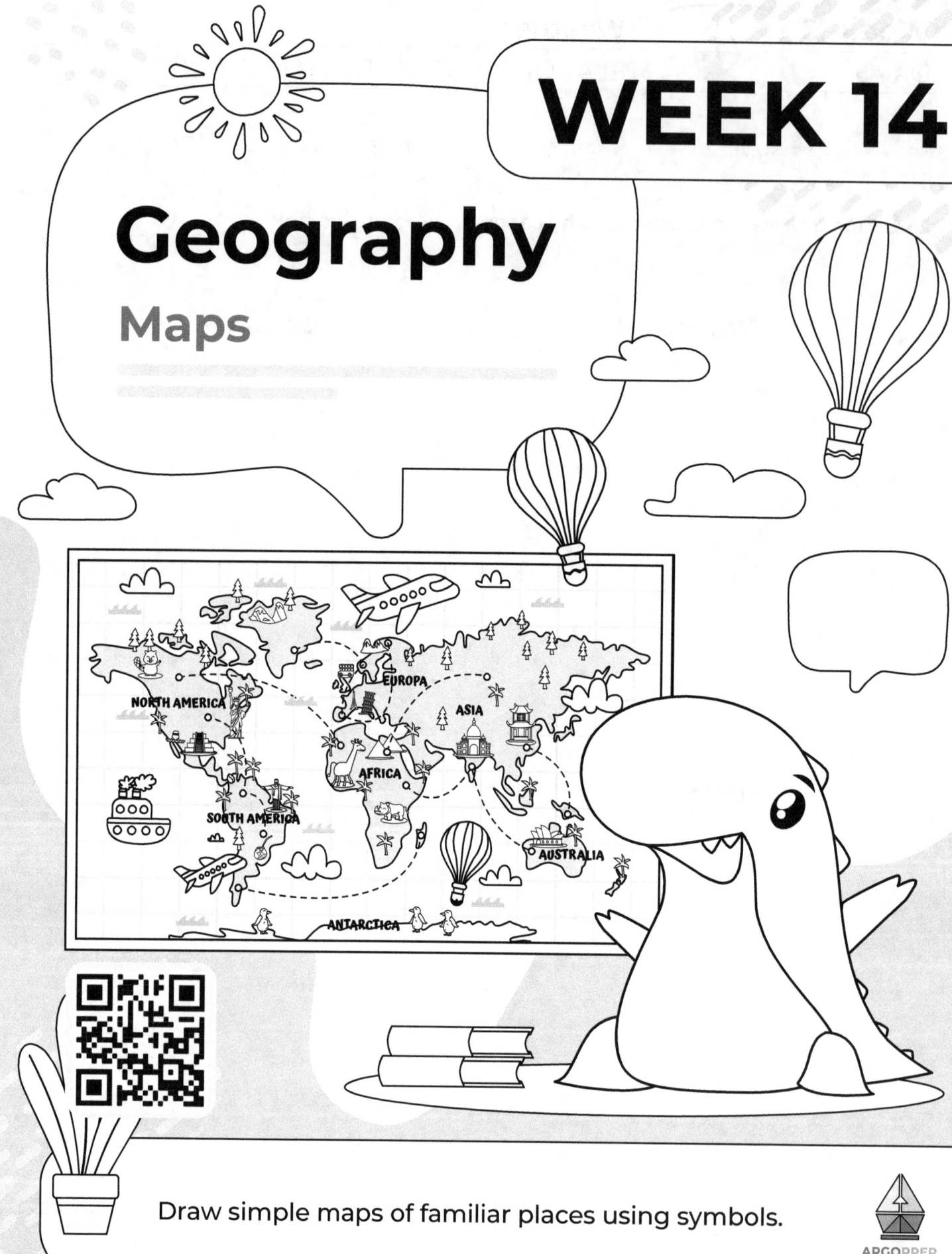

WEEK 14

Geography

Maps

Draw simple maps of familiar places using symbols.

Directions: Read the text below. Then answer the questions that follow.

Maps

A **map** is a flat drawing of a specific place. Maps are used to help us find different places. For instance, a map of a neighborhood might show us where a park, school, or post office can be found. Maps have **symbols** that show where things are. Symbols are drawings that stand for something real. For example, a small blue building may be used as the symbol on a map to represent a bank. Map symbols help us to locate specific places on maps.

1. Maps help people to know where places are located.

   A. True

   B. False

2. Most maps have symbols.

   A. True

   B. False

3. Which statements are true about map symbols? Circle all that apply.

   A. Map symbols show where things are.

   B. Map symbols are small drawings.

   C. Map symbols are always in the shape of a house.

   D. Map symbols stand for something real.

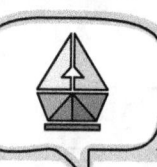
Yesterday you learned about maps and map symbols. Today you will learn more about how map symbols are used.

Directions: Read the text below. Then answer the questions that follow.

> Maps use symbols, or small drawings, to represent something real. These symbols are helpful in locating places on a map. For instance, a group of trees found on a map may represent a forest. There is usually a **map key** or **legend** that helps the reader to know what each symbol stands for.

Directions: Review the map key below. Fill in what each symbol might represent on the line next to the symbol.

Map Key

 ....

 ....

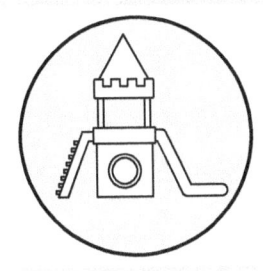

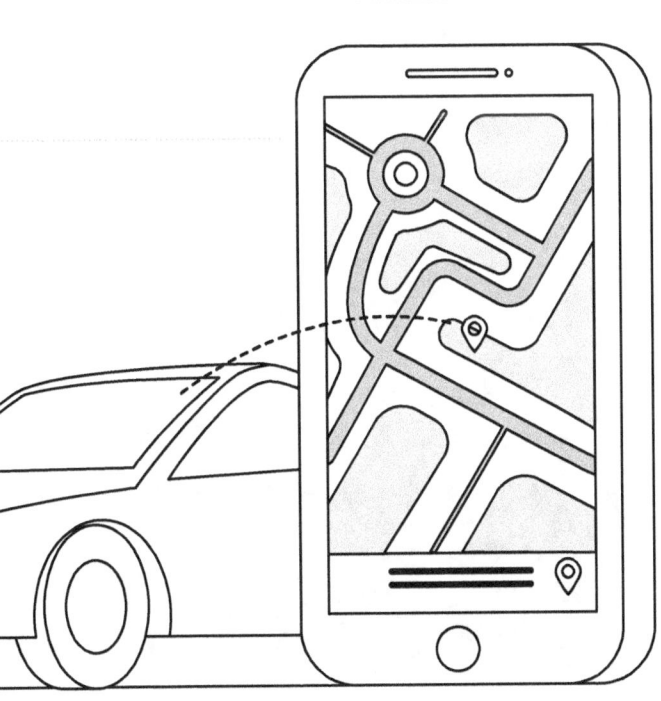

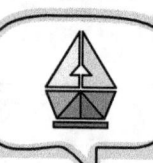
Yesterday you learned more about map symbols. Today you will create your own map symbol and explain what it represents.

Directions: Create a map symbol in the box below. Then complete the sentence that follows.

Map Key

The   symbol   I   drew   was   a

_____

_____ .

It stands for _____ **on a map.**

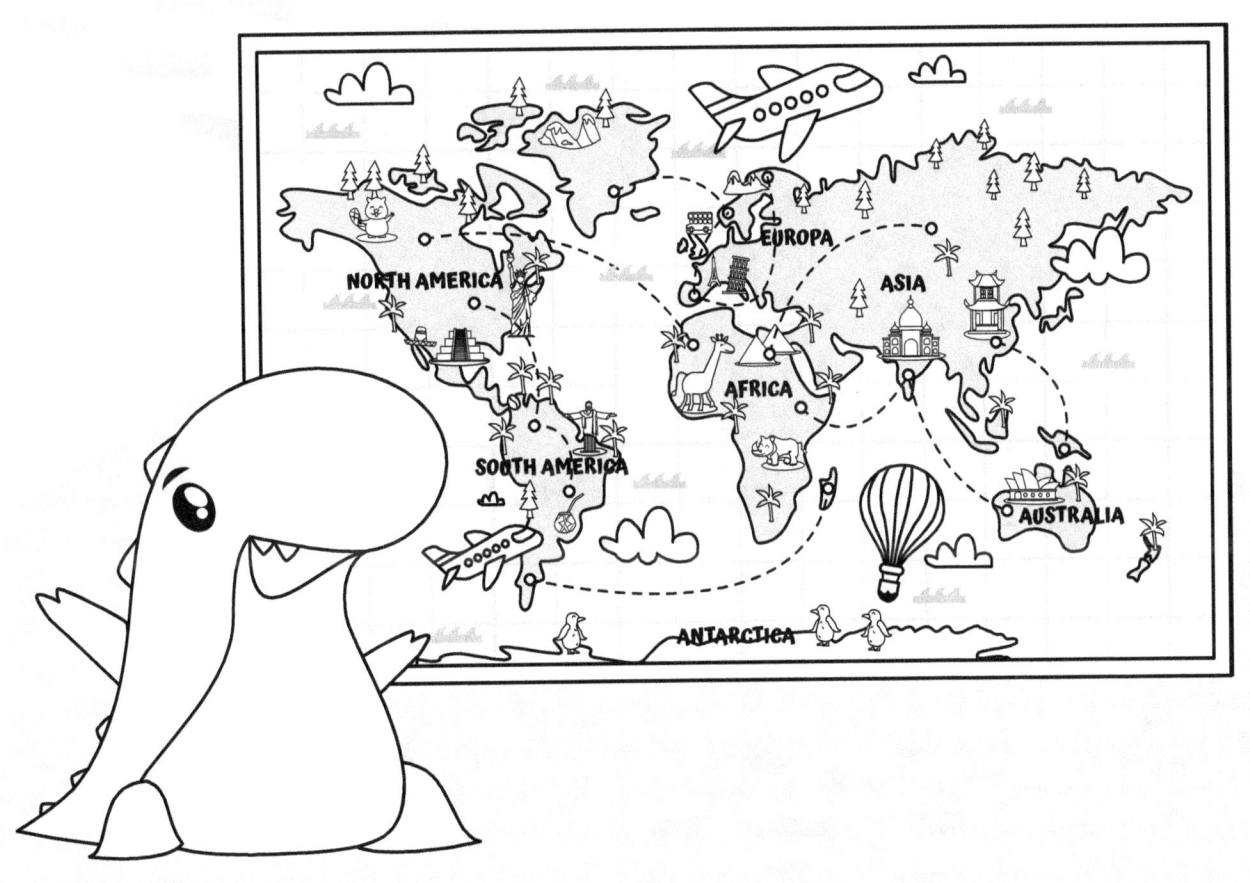

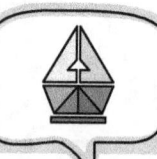
You have spent several days learning, exploring, and explaining what map symbols are. Today you will draw your own map of your classroom, school, or neighborhood.

Directions: Draw a map of your classroom, school, or neighborhood in the box below. Be sure to include a map key.

Yesterday you created your own map and map key. Today you will answer questions about your map.

Directions: Using the map and map key you created yesterday, answer the questions below.

1. What did you draw a map of?

2. How many different symbols did you include on your map key?

3. How will your map key help the reader understand your map?

4. Look at the first symbol on your map key. What does it represent? Why did you choose that symbol?

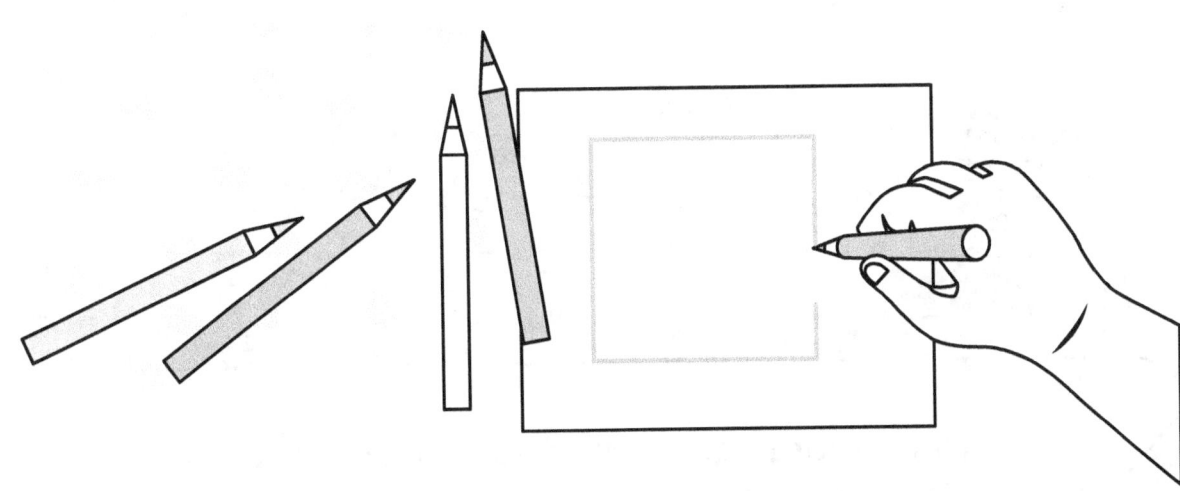

WEEK 15

Geography
Natural Resources

Define natural resources and identify how people use them.

ARGOPREP

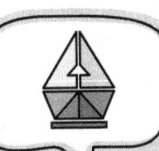
Directions: Read the text below. Then answer the questions that follow.

What are Natural Resources?

Our Earth is full of natural resources. **Natural resources** are things found in nature that people use, such as light, air, water, plants, animals, and soil. Some natural resources are needed to keep people alive, and others just make our lives better. Not all natural resources can be found everywhere in the United States.

1. Natural resources can be found all over Earth.

   A. True
   B. False

2. Which of the following are examples of natural resources? Circle all that apply.

   A. Air
   B. Water
   C. Houses
   D. Plants and animals

3. Which of the following statements are true about natural resources? Circle <u>all</u> that apply.

   A. Natural resources help people survive.
   B. Natural resources are things found in nature.
   C. Natural resources are only needed to make our lives better.
   D. Cars are an example of a natural resource.

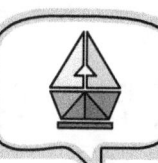
Yesterday you learned about natural resources. Today you will learn more about the difference between natural resources needed for survival and those that make our lives better.

Directions: Read the text below. Then answer the questions that follow.

> Some natural resources are necessary for survival. That means humans must have them in order to live. Examples of this type of natural resource include air and water. Other natural resources are not necessary for survival, but they do make our lives better. An example of this type of natural resource is stone. While we do not need stone in order to survive, many people use it in a variety of ways in their homes and gardens.

Directions: Read each of the natural resources listed below. Decide whether they are needed for survival or not. Write each word in the correct column on the table.

Word Bank		
Water	Sunlight	Rocks
Diamonds	Sand	Plants & Trees

Necessary for Survival	Not Necessary for Survival

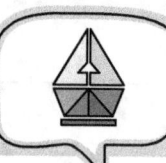
Yesterday you learned more about the difference between natural resources needed for survival and those that make our lives better. Today you will explain why some natural resources are necessary for human survival.

Directions: Choose one of the necessary natural resources from yesterday's activity. Complete the sentences below.

One natural resource that is necessary for human survival is

....

....

This natural resource is necessary for survival because:

....

....

....

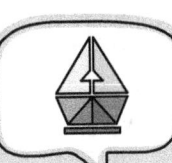
You have spent several days learning, exploring, and explaining what natural resources are. Today you will find out which natural resources are found in the area where you live.

Directions: Using books or the internet, find out which natural resources are found in the area where you live. Write yes or no in the box next to each one.

Water	
Plants	
Animals	
Fossil Fuels	

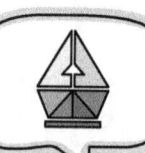
Minerals	
Oil	
Forests	
Soil	

Yesterday you learned about the natural resources found in your area. Today you will write about how those natural resources are used in your community.

Directions: Read the text below. Then answer the questions that follow.

"
Natural resources are used in a variety of ways. For instance, water can be used for drinking, watering plants, and swimming. Thick forests might be used for logging or for enjoyable activities like hiking. Think about the natural resources found in your area. How are they used by people in your community?
"

Directions: Think of a natural resource that is found in your area to answer the questions below.

1. What is a natural resource that is found in the area where you live?

....

....

....

2. List 3 ways the people in your community use this resource.

A. ....

....

B. ....

....

C. ....

....

Economics

Goods

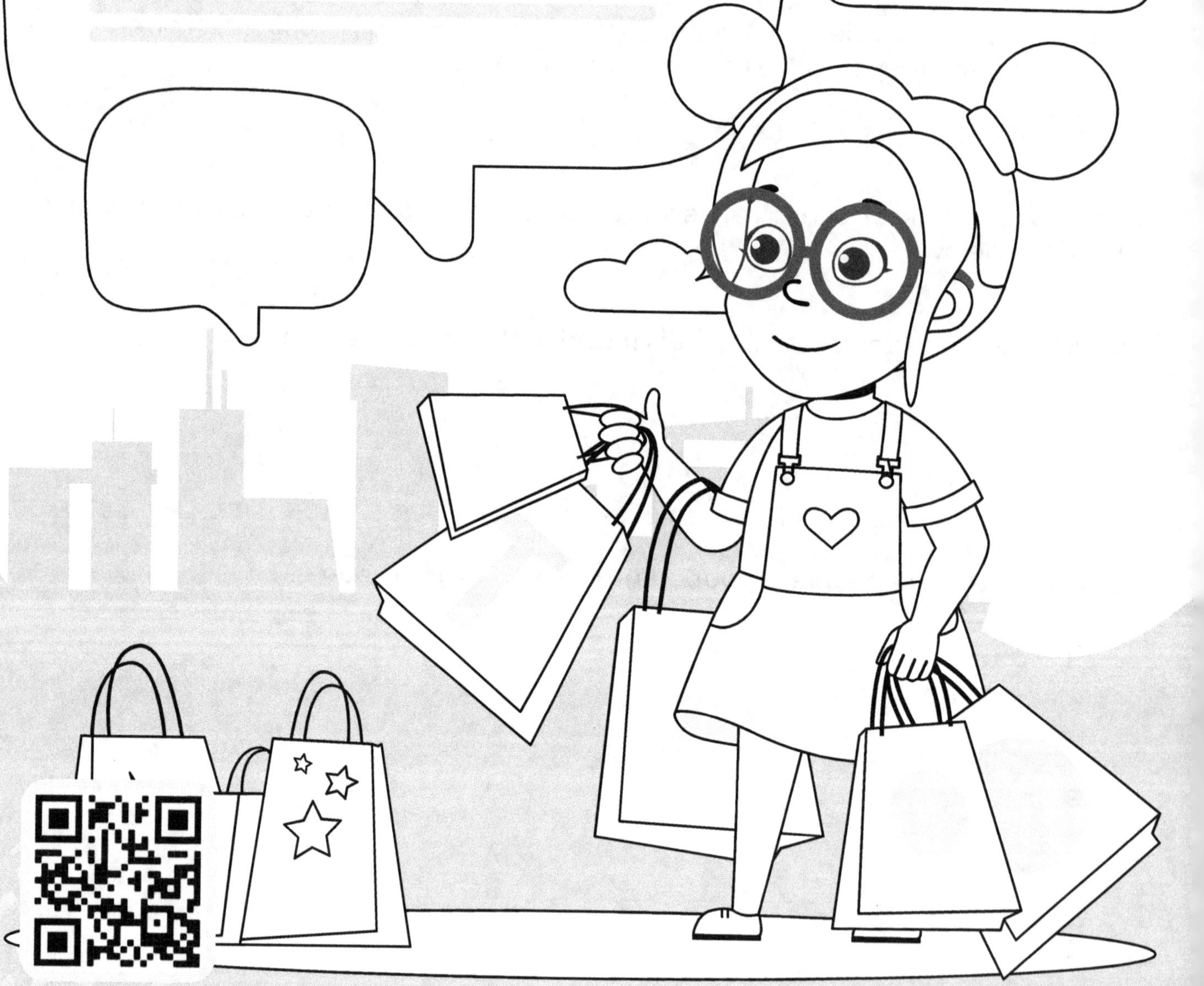

Identify goods that people use.

Directions: Read the text below. Then answer the questions that follow.

Goods

Goods are tangible, or touchable, things that people use in their daily lives. Some goods are necessary for survival like food, while others, such as toys and electronics, satisfy people's wants. Goods usually have to be bought at a store in exchange for **currency**, which is another word for money.

1. All goods are necessary for human survival.

   A. True

   B. False

2. Which of the following are examples of goods? Circle all that apply.

   A. Food

   B. Trees

   C. Cars

   D. Houses

3. In the United States, goods are most often traded for money.

   A. True

   B. False

4. Where are most goods found?

   A. Outdoors

   B. In homes

   C. In stores

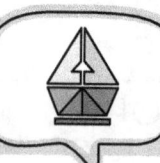
Yesterday you learned about goods. Today you will learn more about the goods that people use on a daily basis.

Directions: Read the text below. Then answer the questions that follow.

> People use many goods on a regular basis. Think about your morning routine. Do you get dressed, brush your teeth, and eat breakfast each morning? Clothing, toothbrushes, and food are all examples of goods that you use each morning. What other goods do you use throughout the day?

Directions: On the table below, list as many goods as you can think of that you use throughout the day.

Goods I Use Each Day

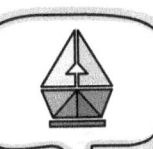
Yesterday you brainstormed all the different goods you use each day. Today you will explain which of these goods are needs and which are wants.

Directions: Read the text below. Then answer the questions that follow.

> Some of the goods people use each day are necessary for survival. For example, food, shelter, and clothing are all needs. People need these things in order to live and function. Other goods are wants, meaning things that provide enjoyment and entertainment. Wants make our lives better in some way. Examples of goods that are wants would be electronics, toys, and games.

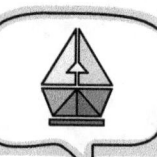
Directions: Using the list you created yesterday, decide which of the goods you use are wants and which are needs. Complete the table below.

Wants	Needs

You have spent several days learning, exploring, and explaining what goods are. Today you will think more about the goods you use each day.

Directions: Think about the goods you use each day. If you were going on a trip and could only take 10 goods with you, what would they be? Fill out the table below with 5 wants and 5 needs.

Wants	Needs

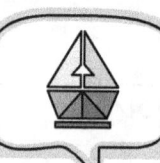
Yesterday you decided which goods are most important to you. Today you will write about why those goods are most important to you.

Directions: Use your lists from yesterday to answer the questions below.

1. Look at your list of 5 wants from yesterday. Why did you choose those items?

_____

_____

_____

_____

_____

_____

2. Look at your list of 5 needs from yesterday. Why did you choose those items?

....

....

....

....

....

....

WEEK 17

Economics

Services

Identify services people do for one another.

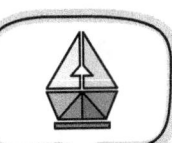
Directions: Read the text below. Then answer the questions that follow.

Services

   Services are actions that people do for others. Sometimes people are paid to provide the service, and other times they are not. Services make our lives better and help us to get things done that we don't know how to do ourselves. Examples of people who provide a service include: mechanics, doctors, plumbers, and firefighters.

1. Some people are paid to provide a service.

   A. True

   B. False

2. Which of the following are examples of people who provide services? Circle all that apply.

   A. Mail carrier

   B. Pilot

   C. Police officer

   D. Teacher

3. Services help us do things we don't know how to do ourselves.

   A. True

   B. False

4. Goods and services are the same thing.

   A. True

   B. False

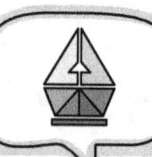
Yesterday you learned about services. Today you will learn more about the services that people use on a daily basis.

> People use many services on a regular basis. Think about a typical day in your family. Does your family sometimes hire a plumber or have groceries delivered? Do you visit the doctor or dentist throughout the year? Plumbers, delivery people, and doctors are all examples of people who provide services that your family might use on a regular basis. What other services does your family use?

Directions: In the table below, list as many services as you can think of that your family uses.

Services My Family Uses

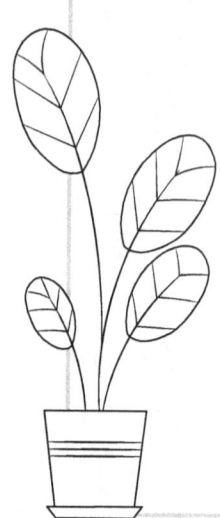

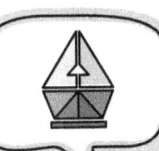
Yesterday you brainstormed all the different services your family regularly uses. Today you will explain which of these services are needs and which are wants.

Directions: Read the text below. Then answer the questions that follow.

> Some of the services people use are necessary for survival. For example, visits to the doctor might be necessary when we are sick and need help getting better. Other services are wants, meaning things that provide enjoyment since they make our lives better in some way. Examples of services that are wants would include visits to a hairdresser or a restaurant.

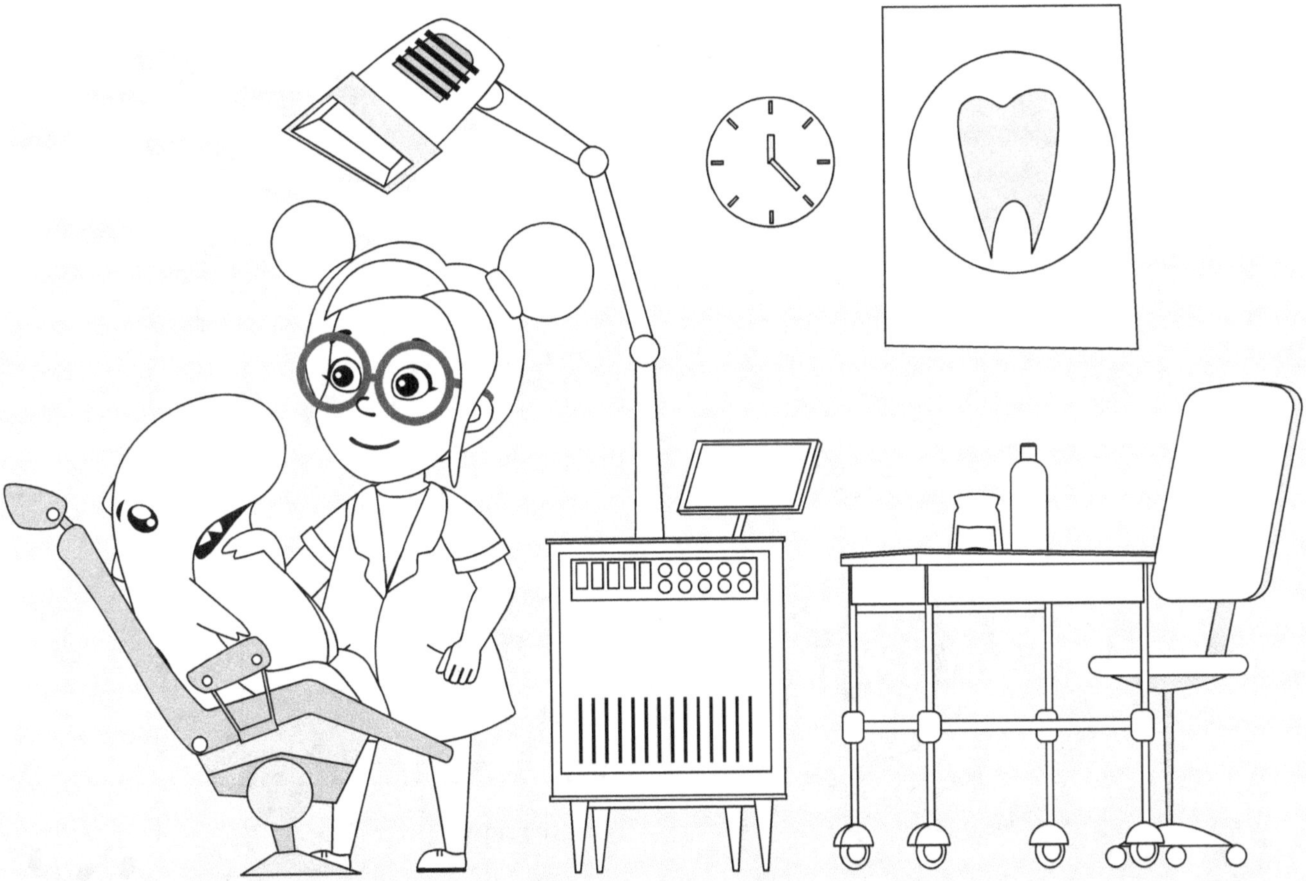

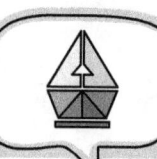
Directions: Using the list you created yesterday, decide which of the services you use are wants and which are needs. Complete the table below.

Wants	Needs

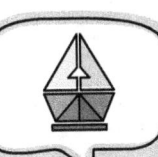
You have spent several days learning, exploring, and explaining what services are. Today you will think more about the services your family uses.

Directions: Think about the services you use each day. Which services are the most important to you and your family and which are the least important? Fill out the table below.

Most Important	Least Important

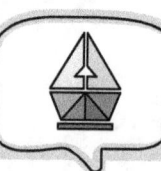
Yesterday you decided which services are most important to you and your family. Today you will write about why those services are most important to you.

Directions: Use your lists from yesterday to answer the questions below.

1. Look at your list of most important services from yesterday. Why did you choose them?

....

....

....

....

....

....

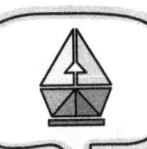
2. Look at your list of least important services from yesterday. Why did you choose them?

....

....

....

....

....

....

WEEK 18

Economics
Producers and Consumers

Sweet Cloud

Sweet Cloud

Describe how people are both producers and consumers.

ARGOPREP

Directions: Read the text below. Then answer the questions that follow.

Producers and Consumers

Producers and consumers play important roles in the economy. **Producers** are people who use resources and materials to make and provide goods and services to others. A baker is an example of a producer. He or she uses a variety of ingredients to make bread or cakes to sell to others. **Consumers** are the people who use these goods and services. In the example above, a person who buys bread from the baker is a consumer. People can be both a producer and a consumer.

1. People can be both producers and consumers.

　A. True

　B. False

2. Which of the following are examples of a producer? Circle all that apply.

　A. Car mechanic

　B. Person who buys clothes

　C. Person who buys food

　D. House painter

3. A person who makes and provides goods and services to others is a:

　A. Producer

　B. Consumer

4. A person who uses goods and services is a:

　A. Producer

　B. Consumer

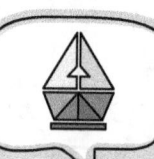
Yesterday you learned about producers and consumers. Today you will learn more about this concept.

Directions: Read the text below. Then answer the questions that follow.

Producers make and provide goods and services to others. There are countless examples of goods and services, including clothing, food, toys, dry cleaning, and car repairs.

Consumers purchase and use the goods and services provided by producers. Usually, money is exchanged for these things. An example of a consumer is a person who buys groceries or clothing at a store.

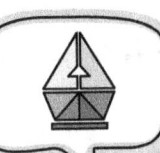
Directions: In the table below, list examples of producers and consumers.

Producers	Consumers

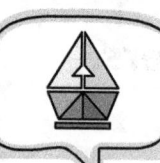
Yesterday you brainstormed a list of producers and consumers. Today you will think of ways that you are a producer.

Directions: In the table below, list examples of how you are a producer.

I am a producer of:

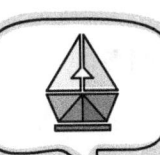
Yesterday you brainstormed ways that you are a producer. Today you will think of ways that you are a consumer.

Directions: In the table below, list examples of how you are a consumer.

I am a consumer of:

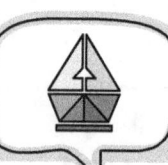
Yesterday you brainstormed ways that you are a consumer. Today you will write more about how people can be both producers and consumers.

Directions: Complete the sentence below.

I know that people can be both producers and consumers. An example of this is: _____

_____

_____

_____

_____

_____

_____

_____

_____

WEEK 19

Economics
Scarcity

Define scarcity and how it affects people's choices.

ARGOPREP

Directions: Read the text below. Then answer the questions that follow.

What is Scarcity?

People use money to exchange, or pay for, goods and services. However, what happens when goods or services are not available or are limited? This is called scarcity. **Scarcity** means there is a shortage of a certain good or service. For instance, if a particular area of a state is expecting a winter storm, certain items such as bread, milk, and eggs become scarce, or difficult to find, at the store because people are buying these things in large amounts. .

1. People usually exchange money for goods and services.

    A. True

    B. False

2. Scarcity means an item is:

    A. Easily available

    B. Limited in supply

    C. Completely unavailable

3. Any type of good could be scarce, depending on the circumstances.

    A. True

    B. False

4. Services can also be scarce at times.

    A. True

    B. False

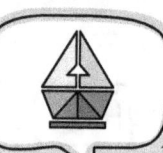
Yesterday you learned about scarcity. Today you will learn more about this concept.

Directions: Read the text below. Then answer the questions that follow.

How Do Goods and Services Become Scarce?

There are several different things that can result in scarcity. Goods can be scarce because too many people want a certain item and there just isn't enough for everyone or because the item cannot be made quickly enough. Services may be scarce because there are not enough people who can provide the service.

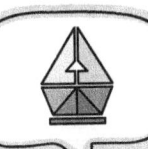
Directions: Complete the sentences below.

1. Scarcity means that there is .... of a certain good or service.

2. Goods can be scarce because .... people want a certain item.

3. Sometimes goods cannot be .... quickly enough.

4. Services can become scarce when not enough .... can provide the service.

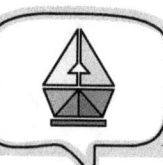
Yesterday you learned about ways that goods and services become scarce. Today you will explain how goods became scarce in a given situation.

Directions: Read the text below. Then answer the questions that follow.

"

It was February in the Upper Peninsula of Michigan. A snowstorm was scheduled to hit late in the day on Tuesday. Schools and offices were closed, and people were rushing to the grocery store to stock up on items. Sometimes when a bad snowstorm happens in this area, it may snow very hard for several days and people are not able to drive on the roads.

Kyle and his mom decided to go to the grocery store on Monday evening so that they would have enough food and necessities at home. When they arrived at the store, Kyle was amazed. He had never seen so many people at the store before! His mom seemed disappointed. She explained to Kyle that when a snowstorm was approaching, people would often buy more than what they needed. This often meant that there would not be enough of certain items for everyone.

As they continued to shop, Kyle understood what his mom meant. The bread aisle was empty. The milk aisle was nearly empty. Kyle and his mom were not able to find everything on their list. They bought what they were able to find and headed home to prepare for the snow.

"

Directions: Answer the questions below.

1. What items were probably scarce in the grocery store?

2. Why were these items hard to find? Why did this scarcity happen?

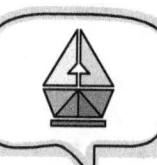
Yesterday you explained how scarcity can happen. Today you will think of ways that scarcity has affected you.

Directions: Write about a time that you have been affected by scarcity.

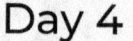

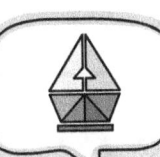
Yesterday you wrote about how you have been affected by scarcity. Today you will write about what can be done when goods and services are scarce.

Directions: Answer the question below.

When goods and services are limited, people have to make choices. What can be done when certain items are limited in supply?

Economics

Jobs

Compare and contrast different jobs people do to earn income.

ARGOPREP

Directions: Read the text below. Then answer the questions that follow.

What is a Job?

A **job** is the work someone does on a regular basis to earn money. There are many different types of jobs people can do. Some jobs require workers to go to college or have special training to learn the skills needed for the job. Other jobs train workers to do the job safely. Workers get paid to do their job. This is how people earn money to pay for their wants and needs.

1. What is a job?

    A. College classes

    B. Special training

    C. Work

    D. Special tools

2. You may need to go to college to do certain types of jobs.

    A. True

    B. False

3. Workers do not get paid for doing their job.

    A. True

    B. False

4. Some jobs require:

    A. College

    B. Special training

    C. All of the above

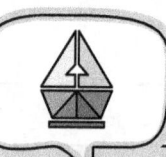
Yesterday you learned what a job is. Today you will further explore the types of jobs people have.

> There are many different types of jobs. Some people have jobs helping or caring for people or animals such as daycare workers, nurses, veterinarians and zookeepers. Some people have jobs providing services like electricians, hairdressers, and mail carriers. Other people have jobs running businesses such as shopkeepers, chefs, or drycleaners. What other jobs can you think of?

Directions: In the table below, list as many jobs as you can think of. You may also draw pictures of the jobs.

What jobs can you think of?

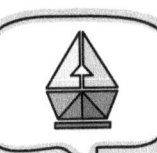
Yesterday you listed different jobs. Today you will choose two of the jobs to compare and contrast.

Directions: Choose two jobs from yesterday's list. Compare and contrast the jobs using the table below.

Job #1: ....

Job #2: ....

How are these two jobs the SAME?	How are these two jobs DIFFERENT?

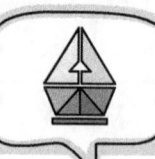
You have spent several days learning, exploring, and explaining different jobs. Today you will read passages and figure out what the character's job is.

Directions: Read each passage. Then decide what job the character has and write it on the line.

1. Charlotte cleans people's teeth. She makes sure their teeth and gums are healthy. What is Charlotte's job?

....

....

2. Sam cuts hair. He uses tools such as scissors, combs, and curling irons. What is Sam's job?

....

....

....

3. Jamie mows lawns and plants flowers and trees in people's yards. He listens to what they want and helps them make their yard look beautiful. What is Jamie's job?

....

....

....

4. Kenny delivers mail and packages to houses. He walks a lot for his job in all types of weather. What is Kenny's job?

....

....

....

5. Jamal makes breads, cookies, and cakes and sells them to customers at his shop. What is Jamal's job?

....

....

....

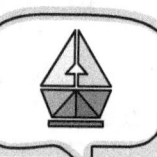
Yesterday you identified the job of a character in a passage. Today you will write about the job you would like to have when you grow up.

Directions: Complete the sentence below. Then draw a picture that matches your sentence.

When I grow up, I would like to be a ....

....

because ....

....

....

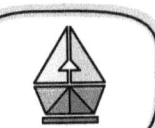

ANSWER KEYS

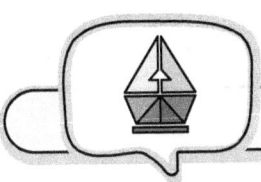

Week 1

Day 1

1. True

2. C, D

3. D

Day 2

Same:	Different
Desks and chairs	One room
Books, paper, and pencils	Blackboard
Teacher	All ages
	Travel far to get to school
	School closed during farming seasons

Day 3

Answers will vary. See Day 2 for possible responses.

Day 4

4. B

5. Answers will vary. (Example: bus, car, walk)

6. Answers will vary.

Day 5

1. Answers will vary. (Examples: people grow their own food, kids attend school)

2. Answers will vary. (Examples: clothing, people drive cars)

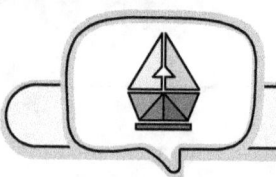

Answer Key

Week 2

Day 1

1. True

2. A, B, D

3. False

4. Answers will vary. (Example: Mount Rushmore)

Day 2

1. True

2. C

3. B

4. President Hoover

Day 3

1. True

2. Answers will vary. (Example: The White House is an important American symbol because it is where our President lives and works.)

Day 4

1. A house

2. Answers will vary. (Example: All the pictures, except the house, show things for which America is famous.)

Day 5

Answers will vary. (Examples: people singing the National Anthem at the beginning of a baseball game)

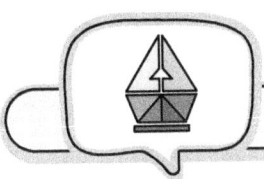

Week 3

Day 1

1. False

2. A

3. True

4. Answers will vary. (Example: Memorial Day)

Day 2

Answers will vary. (Examples: MLK peacefully fought for equal rights for African Americans. MLK was assassinated at a young age. MLK Day is celebrated to honor his birthday.)

Day 3

1. Answers will vary. (Example: Veterans Day is an important national holiday because people in the military risk their lives for our freedoms.)

2. Answers will vary. (Examples: Write a thank you card to a veteran you know. Interview a veteran to learn more about life in the military.)

Day 4

Answers will vary. (Examples: On Independence Day, we go downtown to watch the parade and fireworks.)

Day 5

Answers will vary. (Examples: My new national holiday would be Harriet Tubman Day. It would be celebrated on March 10 which is the day she died because her birthdate is unknown. This would be an important day to celebrate because she was instrumental in helping hundreds of slaves escape to freedom. This holiday could be celebrated with peaceful rallies for racial justice.)

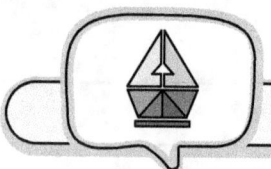

Week 4

Day 1

1. False

2. D

3. True

Day 2

1. 7:20 am

2. Makes his bed

3. Eats breakfast

4. 8:00 am

5. Picture should be of a boy getting dressed or brushing his teeth.

Day 3

Timeline: 1995, 2000, 2013, 2020

1. The events go on the timeline in chronological order. We can figure out the correct order by using the year.

Day 4

Answers will vary. (Example: See timeline example from Day 3)

Day 5

8:15 am - Roberto wakes up.

9:30 am - Roberto opens his birthday presents.

11:00 am - Roberto completes his new building set.

11:30 am - Roberto's birthday party begins.

12:00 pm - Lunchtime

1:00 pm - Roberto opens more presents.

1:30 pm - Roberto's party is over and his friends leave.

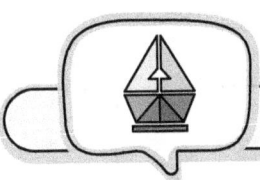

Week 5

Day 1

1. A

2. True

3. B, C

4. C

Day 2

1. The boy, the townspeople

2. The pasture, town

Day 3

1. The moral, or lesson, of the folktale is not to lie because people will not believe you, even when you're telling the truth.

2. I know this is the moral of the folktale because the townspeople did not believe the boy when he was telling the truth because he had lied to them so many times.

Day 4

1. The moral of the folktale is that slow and steady wins the race.

Day 5

Answers will vary. (Example: I felt like Tortoise when a classmate made fun of me for not being a good basketball player in gym class.)

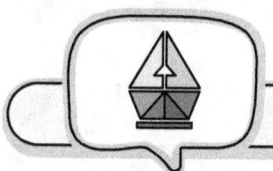

Week 6

Day 1

1. A

2. B

3. A, B, D

4. True

Day 2

1. B, C

2. A, D

Day 3

1. B; This is a responsibility because it is something people should do so that others stay safe.

2. A; This is a right because everyone deserves to live in a safe environment.

3. B; This is a responsibility because it is something people should do to keep our community nice for others.

Day 4

1. You have the responsibility to keep your home clean and safe.

2. You have the responsibility to make healthy food choices.

3. You have the responsibility to care for your clothes.

Day 5

Answers will vary. (Example: I have the right to have clothes. Because I have this right, I am responsible for taking care of my clothes.)

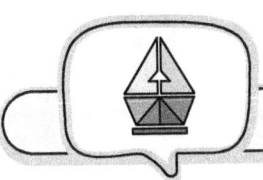

Week 7

Day 1

1. A

2. B

3. A, B, C, D

4. True

Day 2

5. A, B, D

6. B, D

Day 3

Rules:

Raise your hand for permission to speak.

Walk in a single file line in the hallway.

Complete homework before playing.

Laws:

Stop your car at all stop signs.

Do not throw trash on the ground.

Do not take items from a store without paying first.

Day 4

Answers will vary. (Example: Complete homework before playing.)

Day 5

Answers will vary. (Example: Rules and laws are important because they help keep us safe.)

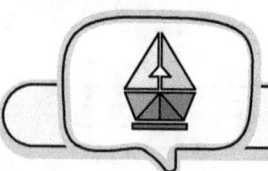

Week 8

Day 1

1. C

2. C

3. C, D

Day 2

1. Yes

2. No

3. No

4. Yes

5. Yes

6. No

Day 3

Action: Bryan and his mom helped raise money for new soccer balls for the gym teacher.

This action was an example of contributing to the common good because every student in the school will benefit from having new soccer balls to practice with in gym class.

Day 4

Answers will vary. (Example: I could pick up litter in the neighborhood park so that it is safe and clean for others to enjoy. Non-example: I could mow my own lawn.)

Day 5

Answers will vary. (Example: Contributing to the common good is important because it helps everyone and makes our community even better.)

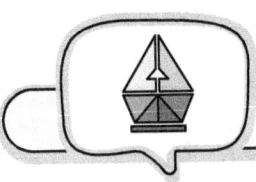

Answer Key

Week 9

Day 1

1. E

2. False

3. A, C, D

Day 2

1. A

2. Answers will vary. (Examples might include: kind, caring, a good friend)

Day 3

1. Answers will vary. (Examples might include: kind, helpful, friendly)

2. Answers will vary. (Example: Cody showed kindness when he agreed to be Julio's helper for the week.)

Day 4

Answers will vary. (Example: I showed good citizenship at school when I cleaned up the entire table after lunch. Non-example: I did not show good citizenship at school when I yelled at my classmate during silent reading.)

Day 5

Answers will vary. (Example: Sharing materials with classmates in art class)

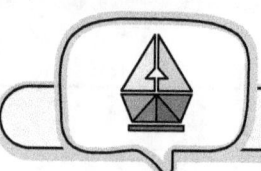

Week 10

Day 1

1. False

2. C

3. D

Day 2

1. B

2. E

3. D

4. A

5. C

Day 3

Answers will vary. (Example: I think The Pledge of Allegiance means we should be loyal to our country and that we should not be divided because the words in The Pledge mean loyalty and togetherness.)

Day 4

Answers will vary. (Example: We recite The Pledge of Allegiance over the morning announcements everyday. Our whole class stands and says it together.)

Day 5

1. I

2. To

3. Of

4. And

5. For

6. It

7. One

8. With

9. And

10. All

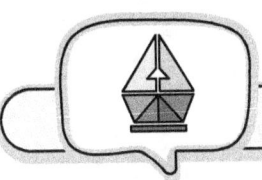

Answer Key

Week 11

Day 1

1. False

2. True

3. B

4. D

Day 2

1. Compass rose

2. Compass

3. Compass rose

Day 3

Answers will vary. (Example: see scenarios from Day 2)

Day 4

Answers will vary. (Example: The library is north of my house.)

Day 5

1. east

2. west

3. west or south

4. park or pond

5. park, pond, library, hospital, and house

6. Everything is east of the pond so students can pick any two things.

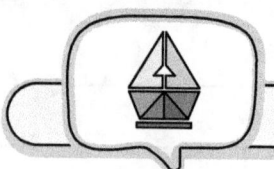

Answer Key

Week 12

Day 1

1. False

2. A

3. B

4. C

Day 2

1. Physical feature

2. Physical feature

3. Human feature

4. Physical feature

5. Human feature

Day 3

1. Nature

2. Answers will vary. (Examples: mountains, river, ocean, land)

3. Humans

4. Answers will vary. (Examples: houses, buildings, farms)

5. The main difference between physical and human features is that one occurs naturally and the other is created by humans.

Day 4

Answers will vary. (Example: Physical features - a river, land and animals, Human features - houses and roads)

Day 5

Answers will vary. (Example: Physical features - mountain, river, ocean, land, plants, animals, Human features - buildings, houses, roads, schools)

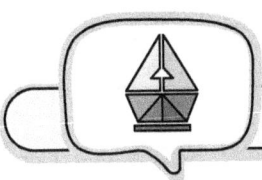

Week 13

Day 1

1. False

2. True

3. A, B

4. Answers will vary. (Example: The weather in winter where I live is cold and snowy.)

Day 2

1. Temperature, precipitation, cloud cover, amount of sunlight

2. Winter, spring, summer, fall

3. Shorter, longer

4. Longer, shorter

Day 3

1. Winter: cold temperatures, lots of snow and clouds, shorter days, longer nights

2. Spring: cool to warm temperatures, rain, longer days, shorter nights

3. Summer: warm to hot temperatures, lots of sun, less rain, longer days, shorter nights

4. Fall: cool temperatures, rain and clouds, shorter days, longer nights

Day 4

Answers will vary. (see Day 3 for sample)

Day 5

Answers will vary.

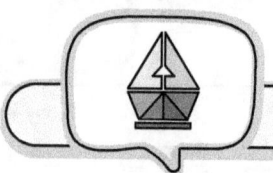

Week 14

Day 1

1. True

2. True

3. A, B, D

Day 2

1. House/neighborhood

2. Airport

3. Library/bookstore

4. Playground

5. Restaurant

6. School bus stop

Day 3

All answers will vary. (see Day 2 for sample)

Day 4

Answers will vary.

Day 5

1. Classroom, school, or neighborhood

2. Answers will vary.

3. The map key will help the reader understand the map by showing where certain things are located in the classroom, school or neighborhood.

4. Answers will vary. (Example: The first symbol on my map key is a picture of a book. It represents the classroom library. I chose that symbol because the classroom library is where all the books are kept.)

Answer Key

Week 15

Day 1

1. True

2. A, B, D

3. A, B

Day 2

Necessary for Survival	Not Necessary for Survival
• Water • Sunlight • Plants & Trees	• Rocks • Diamonds • Sand

Day 3

Answers will vary. (Example: One natural resource that is necessary for human survival is plants. This natural resource is necessary for survival because plants provide the Earth with oxygen and humans need oxygen in order to breathe.)

Day 4

Answers will vary.

Day 5

1. Answers will vary. (Example: forests)

2. Answers will vary. (Example: logging, oxygen, recreation)

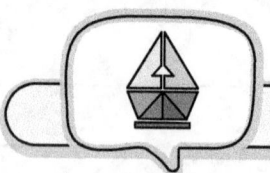

Answer Key

Week 16

Day 1

1. False

2. A, C, D

3. True

4. C

Day 2

Answers will vary. (Examples: food, clothing, toothpaste, pencils, crayons, books)

Day 3

Answers will vary. (Example: wants - pencils, crayons, books; needs - food, clothing, toothpaste)

Day 4

Answers will vary.

Day 5

1. Answers will vary. (Example: I chose those 5 items to take with me because they all have some kind of sentimental value to me.)

2. Answers will vary. (Example: I chose those 5 items to take with me because I don't think I can survive without food, water, medicine, clothing, and soap.)

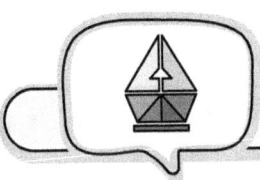

Week 17

Day 1

1. True

2. A, B, C, D

3. True

4. False

Day 2

Answers will vary. (Examples: dry cleaner, dentist, barber, mechanic, librarian)

Day 3

Answers will vary. (Example: wants - dry cleaner, barber, mechanic, librarian; needs - dentist)

Day 4

Answers will vary.

Day 5

1. Answers will vary. (Example: I thought those services were important because they keep my family healthy and safe.)

2. Answers will vary. (Example: I thought those services were less important because we can live without them.)

Week 18

Day 1

1. True

2. A, D

3. A

4. B

Day 2

Answers will vary. (Examples: Producers - seamstress, mechanic, chef; Consumers - a person who needs a carwash, a bride who wants her wedding gown made, a mom or dad who buys groceries at the store)

Day 3

Answers will vary. (Examples: art, lemonade, taking care of younger siblings)

Day 4

Answers will vary. (Examples: food, clothing, toys, electronics)

Day 5

Answers will vary. (Example: I know people can be both producers and consumers. An example of this is my mom who is a producer when she makes food for people to buy at the restaurant she works at and a consumer when she purchases the ingredients for the food from the grocery store.)

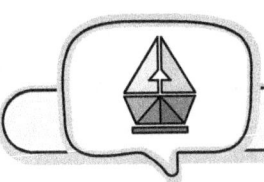

Week 19

Day 1

1. True

2. B

3. True

4. True

Day 2

1. Not enough

2. Too many

3. Made

4. People

Day 3

1. Bread, milk, eggs

2. People overbought certain items. They were afraid they would not have enough to hold them over during the snowstorm.

Day 4

Answers will vary. (Examples: the latest tablet sold out quickly at Christmas, stocking up on essentials prior to a hurricane)

Day 5

Answers will vary. (Example: Buy a different product or find a substitution, use a different product instead, skip it and change the plan)

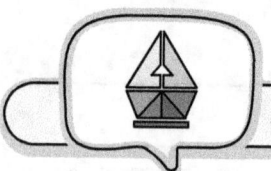

Answer Key

Week 20

Day 1

1. C

2. True

3. False

4. C

Day 2

Answers will vary. (Examples might include: veterinarian, waitress, baseball player, banker)

Day 3

All answers will vary. (Examples might include: A veterinarian and a doctor both help heal. They treat different types of patients, though.)

Day 4

5. Dentist/hygienist

6. Hairdresser

7. Landscaper/gardener

8. Mail carrier

9. Baker

Day 5

All answers will vary.

KIDS WINTER ACADEMY

Kids Winter Academy by ArgoPrep covers material learned in September through December so your child can reinforce the concepts they should have learned in class. We recommend using this particular series during the winter break. This workbook includes two weeks of activities for math, reading, science, and social studies. Best of all, you can access detailed video explanations to all the questions on our website.